SERIES

(ex•ploring)

1. Investigating in a systematic way: examining. 2. Searching
into or ranging over for the purpose of discovery.

Getting Started with

Web Browsers

SERIES

(ex•ploring)

1. Investigating in a systematic way: examining. 2. Searching into or ranging over for the purpose of discovery.

Getting Started with

Web Browsers

Mary Anne Poatsy

Amy Rutledge

Series Created by Dr. Robert T. Grauer

PEARSON

Boston   Columbus   Indianapolis   New York   San Francisco   Hoboken
Amsterdam   Cape Town   Dubai   London   Madrid   Milan   Munich   Paris   Montréal   Toronto
Delhi   Mexico City   São Paulo   Sydney   Hong Kong   Seoul   Singapore   Taipei   Tokyo

Vice President of Career Skills: Andrew Gilfillan
Senior Editor: Samantha McAfee Lewis
Team Lead, Project Management: Laura Burgess
Project Manager: Laura Karahalis
Program Manager: Natacha Moore
Development Editor: Ginny Munroe
Editorial Assistant: Victoria Lasavath
Director of Product Marketing: Maggie Waples
Director of Field Marketing: Leigh Ann Sims
Product Marketing Manager: Kaylee Carlson
Field Marketing Managers: Joanna Sabella
Marketing Coordinator: Susan Osterlitz

Senior Operations Specialist: Diane Peirano
Senior Art Director: Diane Ernsberger
Interior and Cover Design: Diane Ernsberger
Cover Photo: Courtesy of Shutterstock® Images
Associate Director of Design: Blair Brown
Product Strategy Manager: Eric Hakanson
Director of Digital Development: Taylor Ragan
Digital Product Manager: Zachary Alexander
Digital Course Producer: Jaimie Noy
Media Project Manager, Production: John Cassar
Full-Service Project Management: Jenna Vittorioso, Lumina Datamatics, Inc.
Composition: Lumina Datamatics, Inc.

Credits and acknowledgments borrowed from other sources and reproduced, with permission, in this textbook appear on the appropriate page within text.

Microsoft and/or its respective suppliers make no representations about the suitability of the information contained in the documents and related graphics published as part of the services for any purpose. All such documents and related graphics are provided "as is" without warranty of any kind. Microsoft and/or its respective suppliers hereby disclaim all warranties and conditions with regard to this information, including all warranties and conditions of merchantability, whether express, implied or statutory, fitness for a particular purpose, title and non-infringement. In no event shall Microsoft and/or its respective suppliers be liable for any special, indirect or consequential damages or any damages whatsoever resulting from loss of use, data or profits, whether in an action of contract, negligence or other tortious action, arising out of or in connection with the use or performance of information available from the services.

The documents and related graphics contained herein could include technical inaccuracies or typographical errors. Changes are periodically added to the information herein. Microsoft and/or its respective suppliers may make improvements and/or changes in the product(s) and/or the program(s) described herein at any time. Partial screen shots may be viewed in full within the software version specified.

Microsoft® and Windows® are registered trademarks of the Microsoft Corporation in the U.S.A. and other countries. This book is not sponsored or endorsed by or affiliated with the Microsoft Corporation.

Many of the designations by manufacturers and sellers to distinguish their products are claimed as trademarks. Where those designations appear in this book, and the publisher was aware of a trademark claim, the designations have been printed in initial caps or all caps.

Library of Congress Control Number: 2014956881

10 9 8 7 6 5 4 3 2 1

PEARSON

ISBN-10:   0-13-395598-2
ISBN-13: 978-0-13-395598-9

Dedications

To my husband Dan, whose encouragement, patience, and love helped make this endeavor possible. Thank you for taking on the many additional tasks at home so that I could focus on writing. To all my family and friends for their love and support. I want to thank Mary Anne, Laura, Sam, and the entire Pearson team for their help and guidance and for giving me this amazing opportunity.

Amy Rutledge

For my husband Ted, who unselfishly continues to take on more than his share to support me throughout the process; and for my children, Laura, Carolyn, and Teddy, whose encouragement and love have been inspiring.

Mary Anne Poatsy

About the Authors

Amy Rutledge, Author

Amy Rutledge is a Special Instructor of Management Information Systems at Oakland University in Rochester, Michigan. She coordinates academic programs in Microsoft Office applications and introductory management information systems courses for the School of Business Administration. Before joining Oakland University as an instructor, Amy spent several years working for a music distribution company and automotive manufacturer in various corporate roles including IT project management. She holds a B.S. in Business Administration specializing in Management Information Systems, and a B.A. in French Modern Language and Literature. She holds an M.B.A from Oakland University. She resides in Michigan with her husband, Dan and daughter Emma.

Mary Anne Poatsy, Series Editor

Mary Anne is a senior faculty member at Montgomery County Community College, teaching various computer applications and concepts courses in face-to-face and online environments. She holds a B.A. in psychology and education from Mount Holyoke College and an M.B.A. in finance from Northwestern University's Kellogg Graduate School of Management.

Mary Anne has more than 12 years of educational experience. She is currently adjunct faculty at Gwynedd-Mercy College and Montgomery County Community College. She has also taught at Bucks County Community College and Muhlenberg College, as well as conducted personal training. Before teaching, she was Vice President at Shearson Lehman in the Municipal Bond Investment Banking Department.

Dr. Robert T. Grauer, Creator of the Exploring Series

Bob Grauer is an Associate Professor in the Department of Computer Information Systems at the University of Miami, where he is a multiple winner of the Outstanding Teaching Award in the School of Business, most recently in 2009. He has written numerous COBOL texts and is the vision behind the Exploring Office series, with more than three million books in print. His work has been translated into three foreign languages and is used in all aspects of higher education at both national and international levels. Bob Grauer has consulted for several major corporations including IBM and American Express. He received his Ph.D. in Operations Research in 1972 from the Polytechnic Institute of Brooklyn.

Contents

Web Browsers

■ CHAPTER ONE Getting Started with Browser Fundamentals

OBJECTIVES	1
CASE STUDY: FACTORX	1
INTRODUCTION TO BROWSERS	2
Understanding How a Browser Works	2
Opening and Updating Popular Browsers	3
Using Basic Browser Features	7
HANDS-ON EXERCISES	
Introduction to Browsers	11
PERSONALIZE YOUR BROWSER	15
Reviewing and Changing Browser Settings	15
HANDS-ON EXERCISES	
Personalize Your Browser	25
ACCELERATE BROWSING	31
Becoming Familiar with the Favorites or Bookmarks Feature	31
Managing Favorites or Bookmarks	35
Exploring Browser-Specific Accelerators	37

HANDS-ON EXERCISES	
Accelerate Browsing	41
GO BEYOND THE BASICS	48
Improving Browser Functionality with Extensions or Add-Ons	48
Reviewing Security Features	50
HANDS-ON EXERCISES	
Go Beyond the Basics	55
CHAPTER OBJECTIVES REVIEW	59
KEY TERMS MATCHING	60
MULTIPLE CHOICE	61
PRACTICE EXERCISES	62
MID-LEVEL EXERCISES	66
BEYOND THE CLASSROOM	68
CAPSTONE EXERCISE	70
GLOSSARY	71
INDEX	73

Acknowledgments

The Exploring team would like to acknowledge and thank all the reviewers who helped us throughout the years by providing us with their invaluable comments, suggestions, and constructive criticism.

We'd like to especially thank our Focus Group attendees and User Diary Reviewers for this edition:

Stephen Z. Jourdan
Auburn University at Montgomery

Ann Rovetto
Horry-Georgetown Technical College

Jacqueline D. Lawson
Henry Ford Community College

Diane L. Smith
Henry Ford Community College

Sven Aelterman
Troy University

Suzanne M. Jeska
County College of Morris

Susan N. Dozier
Tidewater Community College

Robert G. Phipps Jr.
West Virginia University

Mike Michaelson
Palomar College

Mary Beth Tarver
Northwestern State University

Alexandre C. Probst
Colorado Christian University

Phil Nielson
Salt Lake Community College

Carolyn Barren
Macomb Community College

Sue A. McCrory
Missouri State University

Lucy Parakhovnik
California State University, Northridge

Jakie Brown Jr.
Stevenson University

Craig J. Peterson
American InterContinental University

Terry Ray Rigsby
Hill College

Biswadip Ghosh
Metropolitan State University of Denver

Cheryl Sypniewski
Macomb Community College

Lynn Keane
University of South Carolina

Sheila Gionfriddo
Luzerne College

Dick Hewer
Ferris State College

Carolyn Borne
Louisiana State University

Sumathy Chandrashekar
Salisbury University

Laura Marcoulides
Fullerton College

Don Riggs
SUNY Schenectady County Community College

Gary McFall
Purdue University

James Powers
University of Southern Indiana

James Brown
Central Washington University

Brian Powell
West Virginia University

Sherry Lenhart
Terra Community College

Chen Zhang
Bryant University

Nikia Robinson
Indian River State University

Jill Young
Southeast Missouri State University

Debra Hoffman
Southeast Missouri State University

Tommy Lu
Delaware Technical Community College

Mimi Spain
Southern Maine Community College

We'd like to thank everyone who has been involved in reviewing and providing their feedback, including for our previous editions:

Adriana Lumpkin
Midland College

Alan S. Abrahams
Virginia Tech

Ali Berrached
University of Houston–Downtown

Allen Alexander
Delaware Technical & Community College

Andrea Marchese
Maritime College, State University of New York

Andrew Blitz
Broward College; Edison State College

Angel Norman
University of Tennessee, Knoxville

Angela Clark
University of South Alabama

Ann Rovetto
Horry-Georgetown Technical College

Astrid Todd
Guilford Technical Community College

Audrey Gillant
Maritime College, State University of New York

Barbara Stover
Marion Technical College

Barbara Tollinger
Sinclair Community College

Ben Brahim Taha
Auburn University

Beverly Amer
Northern Arizona University

Beverly Fite
Amarillo College

Bonita Volker
Tidewater Community College

Bonnie Homan
San Francisco State University

Brad West
Sinclair Community College

Brian Powell
West Virginia University

Carol Buser
Owens Community College

Carol Roberts
University of Maine

Carolyn Barren
Macomb Community College

Cathy Poyner
Truman State University

Charles Hodgson
Delgado Community College

Cheri Higgins
Illinois State University

Cheryl Hinds
Norfolk State University

Chris Robinson
Northwest State Community College

Cindy Herbert
Metropolitan Community College–Longview

Dana Hooper
University of Alabama

Dana Johnson
North Dakota State University

Daniela Marghitu
Auburn University

David Noel
University of Central Oklahoma

David Pulis
Maritime College, State University of New York

David Thornton
Jacksonville State University

Dawn Medlin
Appalachian State University

Debby Keen
University of Kentucky

Debra Chapman
University of South Alabama

Derrick Huang
Florida Atlantic University

Diana Baran
Henry Ford Community College

Diane Cassidy
The University of North Carolina at Charlotte

Diane Smith
Henry Ford Community College

Don Danner
San Francisco State University

Don Hoggan
Solano College

Doncho Petkov
Eastern Connecticut State University

Donna Ehrhart
State University of New York at Brockport

Elaine Crable
Xavier University

Elizabeth Duett
Delgado Community College

Erhan Uskup
Houston Community College–Northwest

Eric Martin
University of Tennessee

Erika Nadas
Wilbur Wright College

Floyd Winters
Manatee Community College

Frank Lucente
Westmoreland County Community College

G. Jan Wilms
Union University

Gail Cope
Sinclair Community College

Gary DeLorenzo
California University of Pennsylvania

Gary Garrison
Belmont University

George Cassidy
Sussex County Community College

Gerald Braun
Xavier University

Gerald Burgess
Western New Mexico University

Gladys Swindler
Fort Hays State University

Heith Hennel
Valencia Community College

Henry Rudzinski
Central Connecticut State University

Irene Joos
La Roche College

Iwona Rusin
Baker College; Davenport University

J. Roberto Guzman
San Diego Mesa College

Jan Wilms
Union University

Jane Stam
Onondaga Community College

Janet Bringhurst
Utah State University

Jeanette Dix
Ivy Tech Community College

Jennifer Day
Sinclair Community College

Jill Canine
Ivy Tech Community College

Jim Chaffee
The University of Iowa Tippie College of Business

Joanne Lazirko
University of Wisconsin–Milwaukee

Jodi Milliner
Kansas State University

John Hollenbeck
Blue Ridge Community College

John Seydel
Arkansas State University

Judith A. Scheeren
Westmoreland County Community College

Judith Brown
The University of Memphis

Juliana Cypert
Tarrant County College

Kamaljeet Sanghera
George Mason University

Karen Priestly
Northern Virginia Community College

Karen Ravan
Spartanburg Community College

Kathleen Brenan
Ashland University

Ken Busbee
Houston Community College

Kent Foster
Winthrop University

Kevin Anderson
Solano Community College

Kim Wright
The University of Alabama

Kristen Hockman
University of Missouri–Columbia

Kristi Smith
Allegany College of Maryland

Laura McManamon
University of Dayton

Leanne Chun
Leeward Community College

Lee McClain
Western Washington University

Linda D. Collins
Mesa Community College

Linda Johnsonius
Murray State University

Linda Lau
Longwood University

Linda Theus
Jackson State Community College

Linda Williams
Marion Technical College

Lisa Miller
University of Central Oklahoma

Lister Horn
Pensacola Junior College

Lixin Tao
Pace University

Loraine Miller
Cayuga Community College

Lori Kielty
Central Florida Community College

Lorna Wells
Salt Lake Community College

Lorraine Sauchin
Duquesne University

Lucy Parakhovnik (Parker)
California State University, Northridge

Lynn Mancini
Delaware Technical Community College

Mackinzee Escamilla
South Plains College

Marcia Welch
Highline Community College

Margaret McManus
Northwest Florida State College

Margaret Warrick
Allan Hancock College

Marilyn Hibbert
Salt Lake Community College

Mark Choman
Luzerne County Community College

Mary Duncan
University of Missouri–St. Louis

Melissa Nemeth
Indiana University-Purdue University
Indianapolis

Melody Alexander
Ball State University

Michael Douglas
University of Arkansas at Little Rock

Michael Dunklebarger
Alamance Community College

Michael G. Skaff
College of the Sequoias

Michele Budnovitch
Pennsylvania College of Technology

Mike Jochen
East Stroudsburg University

Mike Scroggins
Missouri State University

Muhammed Badamas
Morgan State University

NaLisa Brown
University of the Ozarks

Nancy Grant
Community College of Allegheny
County–South Campus

Nanette Lareau
University of Arkansas Community
College–Morrilton

Pam Brune
Chattanooga State Community College

Pam Uhlenkamp
Iowa Central Community College

Patrick Smith
Marshall Community and Technical College

Paul Addison
Ivy Tech Community College

Paula Ruby
Arkansas State University

Peggy Burrus
Red Rocks Community College

Peter Ross
SUNY Albany

Philip H. Nielson
Salt Lake Community College

Ralph Hooper
University of Alabama

Ranette Halverson
Midwestern State University

Richard Blamer
John Carroll University

Richard Cacace
Pensacola Junior College

Richard Hewer
Ferris State University

Rob Murray
Ivy Tech Community College

Robert Dušek
Northern Virginia Community College

Robert Sindt
Johnson County Community College

Robert Warren
Delgado Community College

Rocky Belcher
Sinclair Community College

Roger Pick
University of Missouri at Kansas City

Ronnie Creel
Troy University

Rosalie Westerberg
Clover Park Technical College

Ruth Neal
Navarro College

Sandra Thomas
Troy University

Sheila Gionfriddo
Luzerne County Community College

Sherrie Geitgey
Northwest State Community College

Sophia Wilberscheid
Indian River State College

Sophie Lee
California State University,
Long Beach

Stacy Johnson
Iowa Central Community College

Stephanie Kramer
Northwest State Community College

Stephen Jourdan
Auburn University Montgomery

Steven Schwarz
Raritan Valley Community College

Sue McCrory
Missouri State University

Susan Fuschetto
Cerritos College

Susan Medlin
UNC Charlotte

Suzan Spitzberg
Oakton Community College

Sven Aelterman
Troy University

Sylvia Brown
Midland College

Tanya Patrick
Clackamas Community College

Terri Holly
Indian River State College

Thomas Rienzo
Western Michigan University

Tina Johnson
Midwestern State University

Tommy Lu
Delaware Technical and Community College

Troy S. Cash
Northwest Arkansas Community College

Vicki Robertson
Southwest Tennessee Community

Weifeng Chen
California University of Pennsylvania

Wes Anthony
Houston Community College

William Ayen
University of Colorado at Colorado Springs

Wilma Andrews
Virginia Commonwealth University

Yvonne Galusha
University of Iowa

Special thanks to our development and technical team:

Ginny Munroe

Sean Portnoy

Morgan Hetzler

Julie Boyles

Preface

The Exploring Series and You

Exploring is Pearson's Office Application series that requires students like you to think "beyond the point and click." In this edition, we have worked to restructure the Exploring experience around the way you, today's modern student, actually use your resources.

The goal of Exploring is, as it has always been, to go further than teaching just the steps to accomplish a task—the series provides the theoretical foundation for you to understand when and why to apply a skill.

As a result, you achieve a deeper understanding of each application and can apply this critical thinking beyond Office and the classroom.

You are practical students, focused on what you need to do to be successful in this course and beyond, and want to be as efficient as possible. Exploring has evolved to meet you where you are and help you achieve success efficiently. Pearson has paid attention to the habits of students today, how you get information, how you are motivated to do well in class, and what your future goals look like. We asked you and your peers for acceptance of new tools we designed to address these points, and you responded with a resounding "YES!"

Here Is What We Learned About You

You are goal-oriented. You want a good grade in this course—so we rethought how Exploring works so that you can learn the how and why behind the skills in this course to be successful now. You also want to be successful in your future career—so we used motivating case studies to show relevance of these skills to your future careers and incorporated Soft Skills, Collaboration, and Analysis Cases in this edition to set you up for success in the future.

You read, prepare, and study differently than students used to. You use textbooks like a tool—you want to easily identify what you need to know and learn it efficiently. We have added key features such as Step Icons, Hands-On Exercise Videos, and tracked everything via page numbers that allow you to navigate the content efficiently, making the concepts accessible and creating a map to success for you to follow.

You go to college now with a different set of skills than students did five years ago. The new edition of Exploring moves you beyond the basics of the software at a faster pace, without sacrificing coverage of the fundamental skills that you need to know. This ensures that you will be engaged from page 1 to the end of the book.

You and your peers have diverse learning styles. With this in mind, we broadened our definition of "student resources" to include Compass, an online skill database; movable Student Reference cards; Hands-On Exercise videos to provide a secondary lecture-like option of review; Soft Skills video exercises to illustrate important non-technical skills; and the most powerful online homework and assessment tool around with a direct 1:1 content match with the Exploring Series, MyITLab. Exploring will be accessible to all students, regardless of learning style.

Providing You with a Map to Success to Move Beyond the Point and Click

All of these changes and additions will provide you with an easy and efficient path to follow to be successful in this course, regardless of your learning style or any existing knowledge you have at the outset. Our goal is to keep you more engaged in both the hands-on and conceptual sides, helping you to achieve a higher level of understanding that will guarantee you success in this course and in your future career. In addition to the vision and experience of the series creator, Robert T. Grauer, we have assembled a tremendously talented team of Office Applications authors who have devoted themselves to teaching you the ins and outs of Microsoft Word, Excel, Access, and PowerPoint. Led in this edition by series editor Mary Anne Poatsy, the whole team is equally dedicated to providing you with a **map to success** to support the Exploring mission of **moving you beyond the point and click**.

Key Features

- **White Pages/Yellow Pages** clearly distinguish the theory (white pages) from the skills covered in the Hands-On Exercises (yellow pages) so students always know what they are supposed to be doing.

- **Enhanced Objective Mapping** enables students to follow a directed path through each chapter, from the objectives list at the chapter opener through the exercises in the end of chapter.
  - **Objectives List:** This provides a simple list of key objectives covered in the chapter. This includes page numbers so students can skip between objectives where they feel they need the most help.
  - **Step Icons:** These icons appear in the white pages and reference the step numbers in the Hands-On Exercises, providing a correlation between the two so students can easily find conceptual help when they are working hands-on and need a refresher.
  - **Quick Concepts Check:** A series of questions that appear briefly at the end of each white page section. These questions cover the most essential concepts in the white pages required for students to be successful in working the Hands-On Exercises. Page numbers are included for easy reference to help students locate the answers.
  - **Chapter Objectives Review:** Appears toward the end of the chapter and reviews all important concepts throughout the chapter. Newly designed in an easy-to-read bulleted format.

- **Key Terms Matching:** A new exercise that requires students to match key terms to their definitions. This requires students to work actively with this important vocabulary and prove conceptual understanding.

- **Case Study** presents a scenario for the chapter, creating a story that ties the Hands-On Exercises together.

- **End-of-Chapter Exercises** offer instructors several options for assessment. Each chapter has approximately 12–15 exercises ranging from multiple choice questions to open-ended projects. Newly included in this is a Key Terms Matching exercise of approximately 20 questions, as well as a Collaboration Case and Soft Skills Case for every chapter.

- **Enhanced Mid-Level Exercises** include a **Creative Case** (for PowerPoint and Word), which allows students some flexibility and creativity, not being bound by a definitive solution, and an **Analysis Case** (for Excel and Access), which requires students to interpret the data they are using to answer an analytic question, as well as **Discover Steps**, which encourage students to use Help or to problem-solve to accomplish a task.

Instructor Resources

The Instructor's Resource Center, available at **www.pearsonhighered.com**, includes the following:

- **Instructor Manual** provides an overview of all available resources as well as student data and solution files for every exercise.

- **Solution Files with Scorecards** assist with grading the Hands-On Exercises and end-of-chapter exercises.

- **Prepared Exams** allow instructors to assess all skills covered in a chapter with a single project.

- **Rubrics** for Mid-Level Creative Cases and Beyond the Classroom Cases in Microsoft Word format enable instructors to customize the assignments for their classes.

- **PowerPoint Presentations** with notes for each chapter are included for out-of-class study or review.

- **Multiple Choice**, **Key Term Matching**, and **Quick Concepts Check Answer Keys**

- **Test Bank** provides objective-based questions for every chapter.

- **Scripted Lectures** offer an in-class lecture guide for instructors to mirror the Hands-on-Exercises.

Student Resources

Companion Web Site

www.pearsonhighered.com/exploring offers expanded IT resources and self-student tools for students to use for each chapter, including:

- Online Chapter Review

- Glossary

- Chapter Objectives Review

Web Browsers

Getting Started with Browser Fundamentals

Common Browser Features

OBJECTIVES   AFTER YOU READ THIS CHAPTER, YOU WILL BE ABLE TO:

1. Understand how a browser works p. 2

2. Open and update popular browsers p. 3

3. Recognize basic browser features p. 7

4. Review and change browser settings p. 15

5. Become familiar with the favorites or bookmarks feature p. 31

6. Manage favorites or bookmarks p. 35

7. Explore browser-specific accelerators p. 37

8. Improve browser functionality with extensions or add-ons p. 48

9. Review security features p. 50

CASE STUDY | FactorX

You were just hired as a market research assistant for FactorX, a digital marketing and design company that creates interactive applications such as Web sites and computer applications for its clients, usually major corporations. The company is working on a social media marketing campaign for a beverage company. The project will include the creation of a free, online game. A large part of your job will be to research your client's competition, create weekly reports on your findings, and forward the information to the project team. Your research and information will be obtained primarily through the Web and its resources. During the interview, you were asked about your academic record, work experience, and Web know-how. It was during the hands-on performance segment of the interview that your familiarity with several browsers and search engines enabled you to locate the targeted information quickly. This, along with your ability to provide a quick and accurate synopsis of your findings using a variety of application programs and to answer basic questions on Web security and privacy, impressed the interview panel participants, who awarded you the position.

You are excited to get started, contact the project team for its information, research the use of the Internet and social networking sites by other related businesses, and begin to use your knowledge of browsers and the Web to search, bookmark, tag, and pin Web sites. Your browsing knowledge will complement your research skills and lead to the discovery of valuable information that may influence the company's direction and inevitable success.

Introduction to Browsers

The terms *Internet*, *Web*, *Web page*, *browser*, and *Web server* are frequently interchanged and often seem to refer to the same experience. Actually, they are very different. The ***Internet*** consists of thousands of privately and publicly owned computers and networks that grow and interconnect over time into one giant network. The most common way to explain the Internet is that it is a network of networks, the backbone that consists of the hardware over which your data and information travels when you are connected to it. The ***Web*** is a subset of the Internet and is the general term for the content available over the Internet. More specifically, a ***Web page*** refers to an individual document or resource created using established standards, which is transported over the Internet—similar to your car traveling over a highway or your voice traveling across a telephone line. Lastly, the ***browser*** is a program stored on your computer that accesses a ***Web server***, a computer with special software installed that enables it to respond to a browser's request for a Web page. When your browser connects to the Web server that stores your requested page, it pulls a copy of that Web page through the Internet to your system where it then interprets that page, making it appear in a readable format on your computer or mobile device (see Figure 1.1).

In this section, you will learn how a browser works, the importance of knowing your browser's version, and the reasons to keep your browser current. You also will become familiar with some of the basic features that popular browsers share.

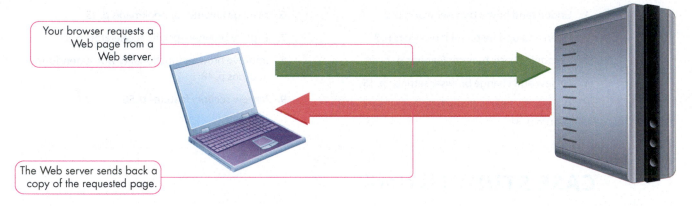

Your browser requests a Web page from a Web server.

The Web server sends back a copy of the requested page.

FIGURE 1.1 How a Browser Works

Understanding How a Browser Works

Web pages are produced using established standards, languages, and styles that create the effects you see when you view a Web page.

HTML is the Web programming language that tells the browser how to present the content on a Web page, such as a link, table, or image. In addition, scripting languages, such as JavaScript, are used along with HTML to make a Web page interactive, such as when you miss a required field in a form and are notified of the oversight by an alert box. Web pages gain more responsiveness when XHR (XMLHttpRequest) is introduced into JavaScript, enabling individual portions of a Web page to be altered without reloading the entire page. Finally when CSS (Cascading Style Sheets) is added to a Web page or all pages in a ***Web site***, a collection of related Web pages, consistent formatting of color, gradients, animation, and overlaid images is facilitated. Web developers refer to this powerful combination of HTML, JavaScript, XHR, CSS, and other Web technologies as AJAX (Asynchronous JavaScript and XML).

The programmers, developers, and companies that create these technologies for the Web also have to ensure that Web browsers support them in order to create a seamless connection between the construction and the display of a Web page. Your browser has to be able to request a page, receive that page, and interpret all of the technologies used within that page to present the final, readable product on your screen, the Web page.

Opening and Updating Popular Browsers

Often when you purchase a new computer, a browser is already installed. If you would rather use a different browser, you can download the current version of a browser from its developer's Web page. Many users have several browsers installed on their system. One does not interfere with another. Both Web developers and Web users find that some Web pages render differently on different browsers and may choose to view pages from different sources in different browsers. That choice comes with experience. Because the toolkits that Web developers use to create Web pages are constantly being upgraded and new programs added, browsers that interpret the code created with these tools also need to be upgraded in order to guarantee that the rendering of the Web page appears true to the developer's intent. For this reason, browsers are regularly updated and distributed for free by developers. Actually, once installed on your system, a browser can be set to automatically update when a new version is detected. Figure 1.2 shows the four most popular browsers as of August 2014. A short clarification around the content of Figure 1.2 might be in order. Popularity and usage polls, when it comes to browsers, seem to contradict each other. Even though the Chrome browser seems to have the largest share of the market in this poll, other polls may count users and usage differently.

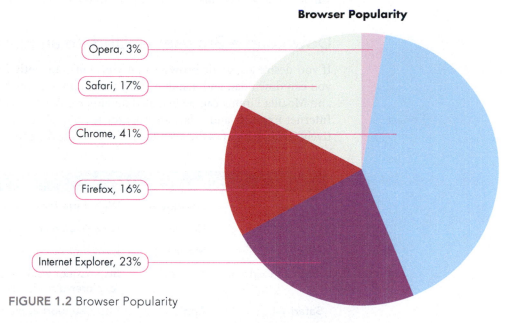

Browser Popularity

Opera, 3%
Safari, 17%
Chrome, 41%
Firefox, 16%
Internet Explorer, 23%

FIGURE 1.2 Browser Popularity

Open a Browser

After you start your system, you need to open your browser. Popular browsers can be identified by a specific icon (see Table 1.1). The first step to opening a browser is to locate it on your system. This can be done in several ways.

- If one of the browser icons appears on your desktop, double-click the icon to open that browser.
- If a browser icon is not on your desktop and you are using a Windows 8 computer, it might appear in your Apps menu. Click the icon to open the browser.
- If a browser icon is not on your desktop and you are using a PC with an earlier version of Windows, it might appear in the Quick Launch Toolbar located on the left side of the taskbar. Clicking the icon on the Quick Launch Toolbar will open the browser.
- If an icon does not appear on your desktop or the Quick Launch Toolbar, locate the browser by name, or icon, in the Start menu or the All Programs menu. Once located, click the browser's name or icon to open it.

TABLE 1.1 Icons Associated with Popular Browsers

Browser Icons			
Chrome	Firefox	Internet Explorer	Safari
Grzegorz knec/Alamy	PSL Images/Alamy	Ivary Inc./Alamy	2020WEB/Alamy

After you open your browser and correctly set up an account with an *Internet service provider*, a company that provides access to the Internet, your browser will open and display your *home page*, the default page presented every time your browser is opened. The home page is set during the installation of your browser and can be changed after installation. You will learn how to change the home page in the next section.

Download a Browser or Update an Existing Browser

If you desire a specific browser that you don't currently have installed on your computer, you can download and install it from the Internet. Some browsers such as Google Chrome and Mozilla Firefox can be installed on either a Windows PC or a Mac, while others such as Internet Explorer and Safari are only for specific platforms, Windows PCs and Mac respectively. Table 1.2 shows the Web Pages for downloading these popular browsers.

TABLE 1.2 Popular Browsers

Browser	Developer	Web Page for Download
Chrome	Google	www.google.com/chrome
Firefox	Mozilla	www.mozilla.org/en-US/firefox/fx/
Internet Explorer	Microsoft	http://windows.microsoft.com/en-US/internet -explorer/downloads/ie
Safari	Apple	http://support.apple.com/downloads/#safari

Browsers are updated frequently. Once you have installed a browser, you should keep it up-to-date. Most popular browsers offer automatic updates to keep you current. Others may give you an option to update when you check their version.

Are there any instances when you should not update a browser? To keep abreast with technology and have a system that runs smoothly and securely you should keep all of your programs and hardware current. However, you may not want to upgrade if there are certain websites that you use frequently and a specific browser version is required. For example, some companies use proprietary web-based systems and the company may not update their system as quickly as the browser is updated.

Identify a Browser's Version

STEP 1 Once a browser is installed on your system, updates to the browser software occur periodically. These updates often provide additional security features and can guard against the most current phishing and malware attempts. Updates also install the newest features of the Web development tools so Web pages will display at their best.

How do you detect the browser version installed on your system? Using Google Chrome as an example, the browser's version can be identified as shown in Figure 1.3, and by following the steps below.

- Open the Chrome browser.
- Google will open and display your home page.
- Click the Google *Customize and control Google Chrome* button, a button with three black lines located in the top-right corner of the browser's window. The Customize and control Google Chrome button replaces the *menu bar*, a horizontal bar positioned across the top of the browser window that contains commands such as File, Edit, View, History, Bookmarks, Tools, and Help. When the Customize and control Google Chrome button is clicked, a menu displaying additional options appears.
- Click About Google Chrome on the menu. A tab will open and display the version of Chrome installed on your system.

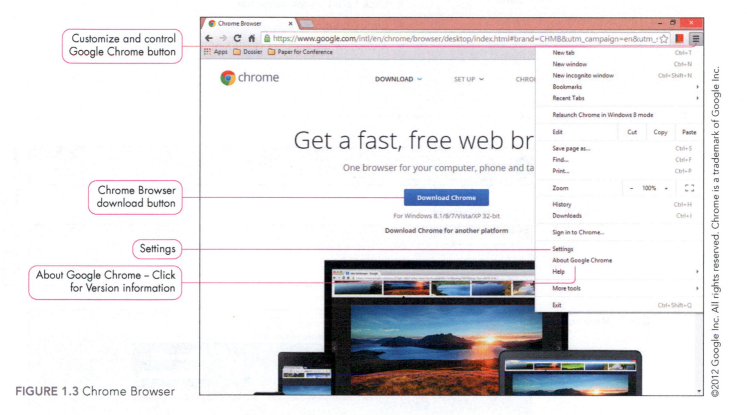

FIGURE 1.3 Chrome Browser

If using a popular browser other than Chrome, see Table 1.3 for directions on locating the browser's version and Figure 1.4 to locate the icons for respective browsers.

TABLE 1.3	Locating a Browser's Version
Browser	**Steps to Menu Locate the Browser's Version**
Firefox	• Click the *Open Menu* button (a button with three black lines) in the top-right corner of the browser's window. • Click the *Help* button (a blue question mark) • Click *About Firefox* on the Help menu. • A window will display, containing the version of Firefox installed.
Internet Explorer	• Click the *Tools* icon in the top-right corner of the browser's window or press *Alt+X*. • Click *About Internet Explorer.* • A window displays the version of Internet Explorer installed.
Safari	• Click *Safari* on the menu bar. • Click *About Safari.* • A window displays the version of Safari installed.

Internet Explorer's Tools icon

Mozilla Firefox's Open Menu Button

Safari's Menu bar

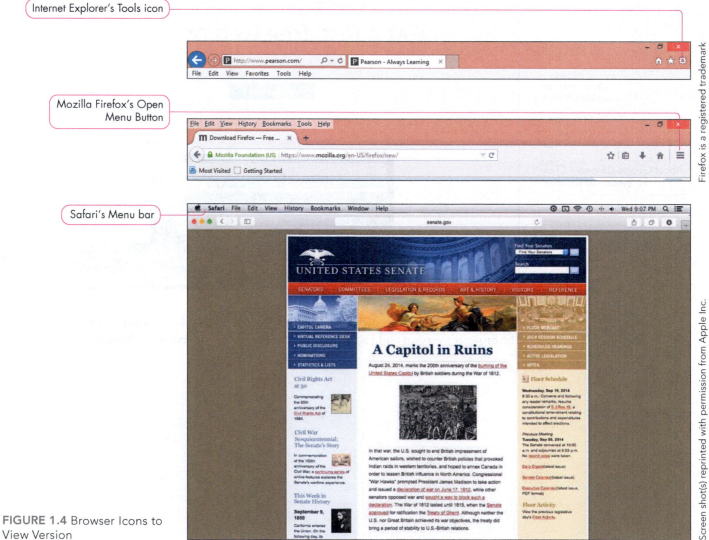

Firefox is a registered trademark of the Mozilla Foundation

Screen shot(s) reprinted with permission from Apple Inc.

FIGURE 1.4 Browser Icons to View Version

Using Basic Browser Features

The popular browsers have a similar interface and many comparable features, such as a Menu or Settings button, a home page, Bookmarks or Favorites, a combined Search/Address/Location box, Forward and Back buttons, a view browser history option, an Open a New Tab button, and the standards such as scroll bars and the Minimize, Maximize, and Close buttons. They may not be in the same location in each browser or get activated in the same way, but they are features that most users interact with when browsing the Web and are available on all browsers. Internet Explorer has two versions for Windows 8.1, a modern version that is touch friendly and has fewer buttons/icons and the traditional desktop version. Moreover, the Address/Location bar is hidden when surfing the Web in the modern version. This allows for more of the Web page to be displayed on the screen. When Internet Explorer is referred to in this book, any figures and exercises will use the desktop version of the browser rather than the modern version.

Identify Screen Elements

To identify the location and appearance of the common browser features overviewed in this section see Figure 1.5, an image of the Chrome browser. Also refer to Table 1.4 (see page 10) to see whether the feature appears, or can be made to appear, in other browsers. You are probably already familiar with several uniform features that appear in all browser windows:

- The three buttons known as Minimize, Maximize/Restore Down, and Close are located in the top-right corner of all four popular browser windows.
- Scroll bars and scroll arrows are located on the right and bottom of all browser windows.
- The Go back one page and Go forward one page buttons are in the top-left corner of all browser windows. The arrows may vary in appearance but their purpose is the same, to return you to the Web page that was viewed previously or to advance to the Web page that you viewed after the one currently displayed.
- The *title bar* is the thick top border of the browser's window.

Browser features do not always look the same from browser to browser but still behave, or are accessed, in similar ways. Many browsers have Menu or Settings icons that replace a traditional menu bar. A *menu bar* is a horizontal bar positioned across the top of the browser window that contains commands such as File, Edit, View, History, Bookmarks, Tools, and Help. If you prefer the traditional menu bar at the top of your Firefox or Internet Explorer window, you can make it visible by right-clicking on a blank area of the browser's title bar and selecting Menu Bar from the shortcut menu that appears. You cannot hide Safari's menu bar. Chrome actually has no menu bar, but has menu bar commands in the *Customize and control Google Chrome* menu.

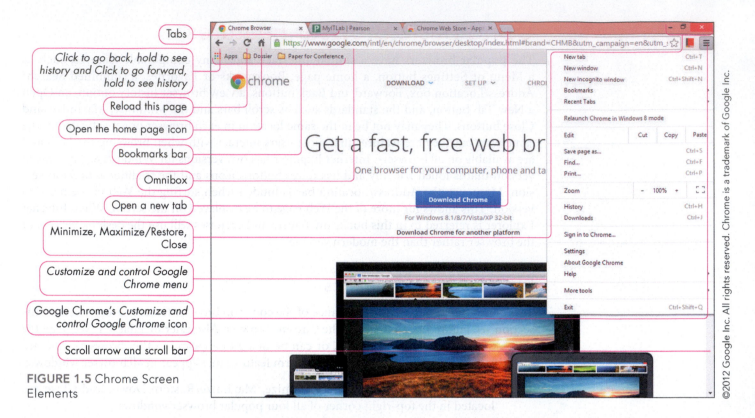

Tabs

Click to go back, hold to see history and Click to go forward, hold to see history

Reload this page

Open the home page icon

Bookmarks bar

Omnibox

Open a new tab

Minimize, Maximize/Restore, Close

Customize and control Google Chrome menu

Google Chrome's *Customize and control Google Chrome* icon

Scroll arrow and scroll bar

FIGURE 1.5 Chrome Screen Elements

STEP 2

Near the top of all browser windows are features to help you access the Web content you want. The ***Address/Location bar*** is the box located near the top of the browser's window. The Address/Location bar is the place you type a ***Uniform Resource Locator (URL)***, also called a Web address, a string of characters that precisely identifies a Web site's type and location. You might notice in most of the current browsers, such as Internet Explorer, Safari, and Chrome, that the address and search bars have been united in order to reduce the interface and make more room to display Web content. This dual-purpose single box is referred to as the ***One Box*** in Internet Explorer, the Omnibar in Safari, and ***Omnibox*** in Chrome and can be used as an Address/Location bar or a Search bar depending on whether you enter a URL or a word related to your search item. The AutoComplete feature also supplies suggestions for the Search box, One Box, and Omnibox. Some browsers, such as Firefox, still display a separate ***Search bar***, a box located near the top of a browser's window, usually to the right of the Address/Location bar, in which you enter words or strings of words related to your search item. Firefox has the ***Awesome Bar***, which enables the user to enter a URL or search term. The browser also has maintained a separate search box.

To utilize the AutoComplete feature, type in the URL of a Web site or a key word associated with the site, such as "bank," and AutoComplete will display possible matches (see Figure 1.6). Click the match from the displayed list or continue to enter the URL if no match appears.

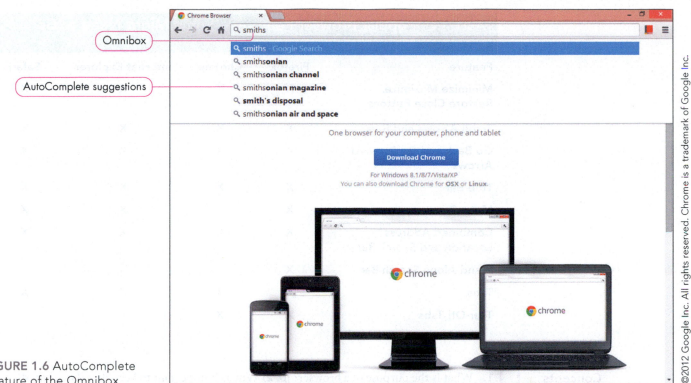

FIGURE 1.6 AutoComplete Feature of the Omnibox

Omnibox

AutoComplete suggestions

Make Use of Tabs

STEP 3

All current browsers make use of the *tab* feature. This is the component of a browser that enables you to open multiple Web pages in the same browser window without starting multiple Web sessions. A tab identifies each Web page, and all tabs are aligned in one row near the top of the browser window. In Internet Explorer, tabs appear to the right of the One Box. By right-clicking Internet Explorer's title bar and selecting Show tabs on a separate row, the tabs will appear below the One Box. When you open your browser, your home page opens in the first tab. Additional tabs can be opened in one of several ways:

- In Chrome, Firefox, and Internet Explorer, click the *Open a new tab* (or *New tab*) icon located to the right of the last opened tab.
- In Chrome, Firefox, Internet Explorer, press *Ctrl+T*. In Safari, press *Command+T*.
- In Chrome, click the *Customize and control Google Chrome* icon and select *New tab*.

As you open more and more tabs, the width of each tab will decrease, enabling more tabs to remain visible at the top of the browser's window. However, if all the tabs cannot be displayed, scroll arrows to the right and left of the tab row will appear, enabling you to scroll through all the tabs in use.

Tabs open from left to right in the order you access the Web pages; you can rearrange tabs by simply clicking on a tab and dragging it to a new location in the row of tabs. If a tab is closed accidentally, Firefox and Internet Explorer enable you to undo or reopen a closed tab. To use this option, right-click a current tab and choose *Undo Close Tab* or *Reopen Closed Tab* from the shortcut menu that appears. The last tab closed will re-open in a new tab. Safari can reopen a closed tab by clicking Edit on the menu bar and then clicking Undo Closed Tab. Chrome can reopen recently closed tabs by clicking the Customize and control Google Chrome button then hover over Recent tabs and choose the most recent tab. Chrome, Firefox, Internet Explorer, and Safari all make use of *tear-off tabs*, a feature that enables you to drag a tab off of the tab window and release it, making that tab its own browser window.

TABLE 1.4	Popular Browser Features—Some Might Need to Be Made Visible				
Feature	**Firefox**	**Chrome**	**Internet Explorer**	**Safari**
Minimize Maximize/ Restore Close Buttons	X	X	X	X
Scroll Arrows and Bars	X	X	X	X
Go Back and Go Forward Arrows	X	X	X	X
Title Bar	X	X	X	X
Menu Bar	X		X	X
Combined Address/ Location and Search Bar	X	X	X	X
Stand Alone Search Bar	X			
Tabs	X	X	X	X
Tear-Off Tabs	X	X	X	X

Quick
Concepts

1. What is the purpose of a browser? *(p. 2)* Why is it important to keep it updated? *(p. 4)*

2. List three popular browsers. *(p. 4)*

3. Name four common browser features. *(p. 7)*

4. What is the purpose of a tear-off tab? *(p. 9)*

Hands-On Exercises

1 Introduction to Browsers

In your new position as research assistant for FactorX, you are anxious to get started. You want to identify the browser installed on your desktop, determine its version, experiment with the AutoComplete feature, and learn to use tabs efficiently.

Skills covered: Opening and Updating Popular Browsers • Using Basic Browser Features • Making Use of Tabs

STEP 1 ❯❯ OPENING AND UPDATING POPULAR BROWSERS

You turn on your desktop system and realize that you have several browsers installed. You choose Internet Explorer. Open the browser and determine its version. Refer to Figure 1.7 as you complete Step 1. If a browser other than Internet Explorer is used for this exercise, your results will not be the same as those displayed.

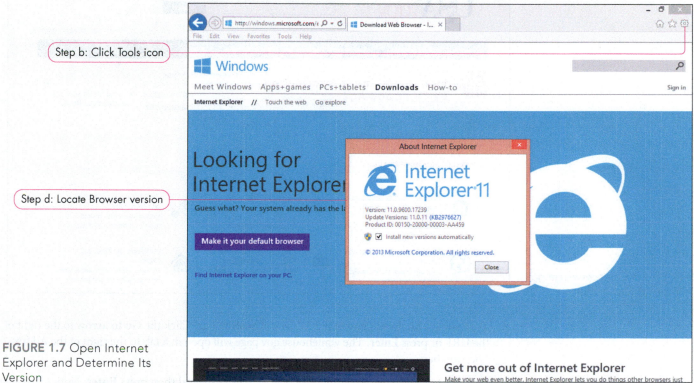

FIGURE 1.7 Open Internet Explorer and Determine Its Version

a. Click **Internet Explorer** on your desktop or taskbar, or select **Internet Explorer** from the Start menu.

b. Click **Help** on the menu bar, and then click **About Internet Explorer**. A window will appear and display the version of Internet Explorer installed on your system.

> **TROUBLESHOOTING:** If the menu bar is not visible, click the **Tools icon**, and then click **About Internet Explorer**.

c. Open a blank Word document, and then on the first line, type **Hands-on Exercise 1**. Press **Enter** and type *your full name* and the *date*.

d. Press **Enter** and type **Version of Internet Explorer:** and the version of Internet Explorer installed on your system, as indicated in the window displays in your browser. Press **Enter**.

e. Click **Close** to close the About Internet Explorer window.

   f. Save the Word document as **wbr01h1_LastFirst.docx**.

   g. Keep both the browser and Word document open.

STEP 2 ›› USING BASIC BROWSER FEATURES

You want to get comfortable with the Address/Location bar in Internet Explorer and decide to open and close a few government Web sites for practice. Your colleagues at FactorX seem to like the AutoComplete feature of the Address/Location bar and Search bar in the newer browser versions. They say it saves time and eliminates the need to remember long URLs. After listening to their advice, you want to give AutoComplete a try. Refer to Figures 1.8 and 1.9 as you complete Step 2.

FIGURE 1.8 Open www.usa.gov in Internet Explorer

   a. Type **www.whitehouse.gov** in the **Address/Location bar**. Click the **Go to arrow** to the right of the URL or press **Enter**. The whitehouse.gov page will open in a tab to the right of the Address/Location bar.

   b. Highlight the URL www.whitehouse.gov, type **usa.gov** and then press **Enter**. Notice that you did not have to enter http://www in front of the URL. Instead, Internet Explorer added this protocol for you.

   c. Highlight the URL www.usa.gov, in the Address/Location bar, type **senate.gov** and then click the **Go to** arrow. The protocol http:// was added by Internet Explorer.

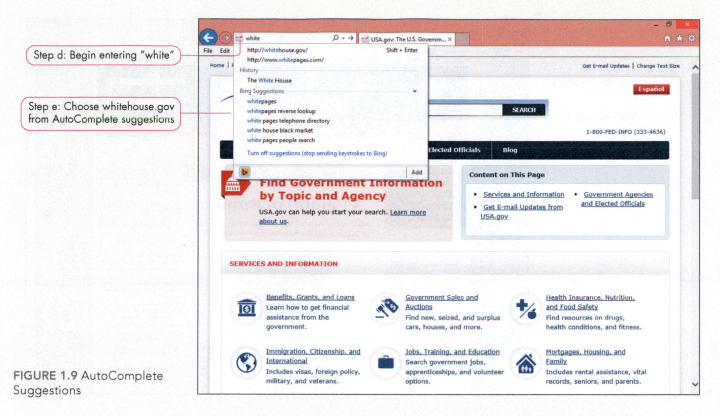

Step d: Begin entering "white"

Step e: Choose whitehouse.gov from AutoComplete suggestions

FIGURE 1.9 AutoComplete Suggestions

d. Type the word **white** in the Addrss/Location bar. These are the first characters of the whitehouse.gov Web site you recently accessed.

AutoComplete produces a list of suggestions below the Address/Location bar.

e. Click the **whitehouse.gov URL** displayed at the top of the AutoComplete suggestion list to go to the Web site.

TROUBLESHOOTING: If the URL of the Web site that you want does not display in the AutoComplete suggestion list, keep typing until it does display or until the entire URL is entered.

f. Type **sen** in the Address/Location bar of Internet Explorer. These are the initial characters of the senate.gov Web site you want to access.

AutoComplete produces a list of suggestions below the Address/Location bar.

g. Click the **senate.gov URL** in the AutoComplete suggestion list to go to the Web site.

Keep the browser window and the tab with senate.gov open and continue to Step 4.

STEP 3 ▶▶ MAKE USE OF TABS

You will often have multiple Web pages open to compare social media campaigns, applications, and marketing strategies of your clients' competitors. You want to practice using Internet Explorer to open additional Web pages in the same browser window. Refer to Figure 1.10 as you complete Step 3.

Step e: Move browser tabs to new locations

Step a: Click New tab icon

FIGURE 1.10 Using and Reordering Tabs

a. Click the **New tab icon,** located to the right of the senate.gov tab, or press **Ctrl+T**.

b. Type **www.bing.com** in the Address/Location bar of the active tab and press **Enter**.

c. Open another new tab.

d. Type **www.nasa.gov** in the Address/Location bar of the active tab and press **Enter**.

e. Drag the **Bing tab** so that it is the first tab. Continuing with this method, rearrange the tabs so that the second tab is the NASA tab and the third tab is the senate.gov <http://senate.gov> tab. Click the Bing tab.

f. Click **Snipping Tool** in the Accessories folder of the Start menu. You will create a snip of your browser's window.

g. Click the **New snip arrow** and click **Full-screen Snip**.

h. Click **File** on the menu bar located in the Snipping Tool window that opens and click **Save As** from the list of File options.

i. Select the drive and folder in which you want to save your image in the Save As dialog box and save it as **wbr01h1_LastFirst.jpg**.

j. Close the JPEG file.

k. Select the Word document **wbr01h1_LastFirst.docx** to make it active.

l. Move the cursor to the end of the Word document and select Pictures on the Insert tab.

m. Navigate to the *wbr01h1_LastFirst.jpg* file and click **Insert**.

n. Click **File** and click **Save**. Close the file and submit based on your instructor's directions.

o. **Close** Internet Explorer.

Personalize Your Browser

Browsers are a large component of everyone's Internet experience. However, everyone that opens a browser does not use all of the same features in the same way or expect the same response to certain behaviors. No matter which browser you choose, you can customize your browsing experience to your individual needs by changing several settings within your browser.

In this section, you will learn where to locate settings to establish a home page, control your browsing history, and confirm the closing of a browser's window that has multiple tabs opened. You will also become familiar with options to restrict cookies and activate Privacy browsing.

Reviewing and Changing Browser Settings

It is helpful to look at the basic browser settings after you download and install a browser. Most browsers have an option or preference setting located within their tools, customize and control, or setting menu. To change the settings in Chrome:

- Click the Customize and control Google Chrome button.
- Click Settings.
- The Settings page will open in a new tab.

To locate options or preferences in other popular browsers refer to Table 1.5.

TABLE 1.5	Locating a Browser's Options/Settings/Preferences
Browser	**Locating the Option/Preference Browser Settings**
Firefox	• Click the *Open menu* button. • Click *Options*. • The Options dialog box will display.
Internet Explorer	• Click the *Tools* icon. • Click *Internet options*. • The Internet Options window displays.
Safari	• Click *Safari*. • Click *Preferences*. • The Preferences dialog box will open.

Each browser displays options differently. If you're using the Chrome browser, the Settings window opens as a Web page in a new browser tab (see Figure 1.11), not as a dialog box as with Firefox or Internet Explorer (see Figure 1.12). A closer look at these settings in the Chrome browser will help you locate features and options that you might want to review or change. As you become familiar with these categories, you will find the categories and the content of the other browsers are similar.

- *Sign in* This setting is a feature that enables you to create a user account that allows you to save your personalized browser features such as bookmarks and access them anywhere on any computer. A Google Account is not required to use the Chrome browser. It is important to note that you don't want to sign in to Chrome if you're using a public or untrusted computer. When you sign in, a copy of your data is stored on the computer and can then be accessed by other people who use that computer. You can delete your data by deleting the user under the *Users* setting (see below).

- *On startup* The on startup setting lets you choose what happens when the browser opens. You can choose to open a new page (for your designated home page), continue on the Web site where you left off when you last used the browser, or open a specific page or set of pages.
- *Appearance* The first option under this setting, *Get Themes*, enables you to customize your browser with various themes. The second option, *Show Home* button, enables you to show a House icon on the toolbar that takes you to your designated home page. The last option, *Always show the bookmarks bar*, enables you to toggle on or off the bookmarks toolbar.
- *Search* The search setting sets which search engine is used when search from the Omnibox.
- *People* This setting enables you to add a new user to the Chrome account, delete a user, or import bookmarks and settings from another browser.
- *Default browser* The default browser setting lets you know whether Google Chrome is your default browser.

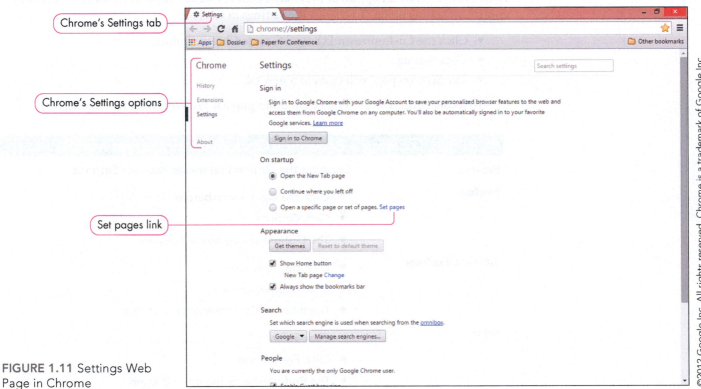

FIGURE 1.11 Settings Web Page in Chrome

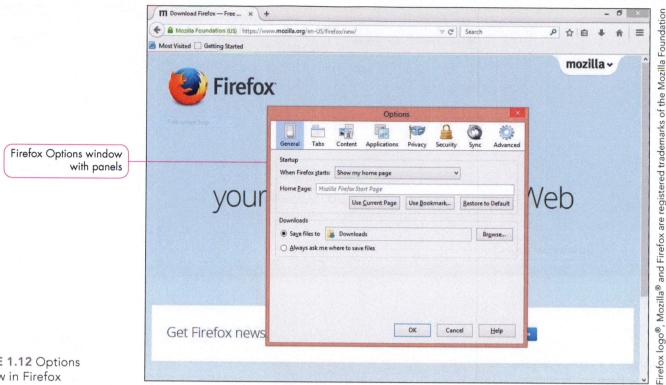

Firefox Options window with panels

FIGURE 1.12 Options Window in Firefox

Set a Home Page

STEP 1 The home page is the default page that automatically displays whenever you open your browser. You can set one or several pages (to open in separate tabs) when the browser is opened. The following steps will assist you in changing your home page settings in Chrome.

1. Click *Customize and control Google Chrome*.
2. Click *Settings*.
3. In the On startup section, if necessary, click the button to the left of the Open a specific page or set of pages option. Then click the *Set pages* link located to its right. The Startup pages dialog box will appear (see Figure 1.13).
4. Type the URL of your desired home page in the Add a new page box or click the Use current pages button and click OK.
5. Instead of displaying the home page of your choice you can change the On startup option to either show a blank page by choosing Open the New Tab page or show the windows and tabs from the last time your browser was opened by choosing Continue where you left off (see Figure 1.14). Refer to Table 1.6 to change the home page of other popular browsers.

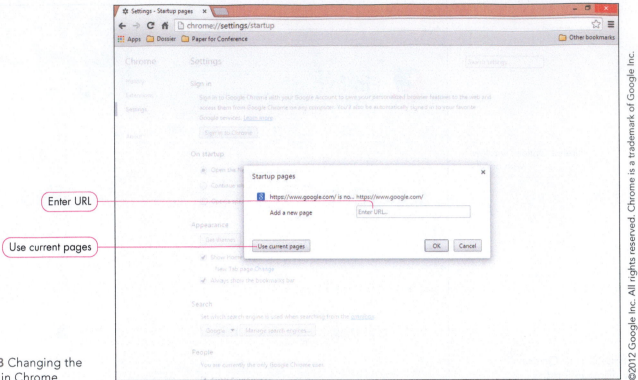

FIGURE 1.13 Changing the Home Page in Chrome

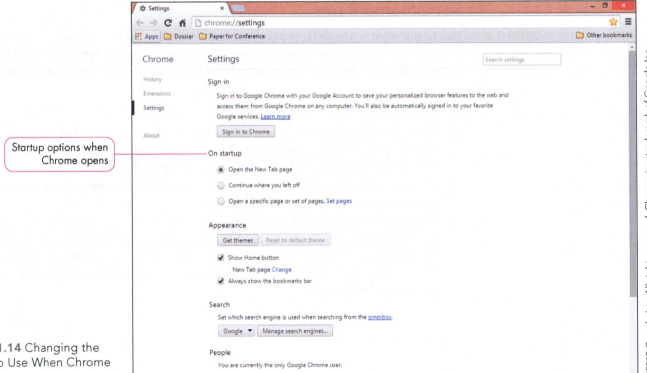

FIGURE 1.14 Changing the Option to Use When Chrome Starts

TABLE 1.6 Setting a Home Page

Browser	Changing the Home Page
Firefox	<ul><li>Click the *Open menu* button.</li><li>Click *Options*.</li><li>Click the *General* panel in the Options dialog box.</li><li>Enter the URL of the Web page you want be the home page in the Home Page box. If the Web page you are currently viewing is the page you want to be your home page, click Use Current Pages.</li><li>Click *OK*.</li></ul>
Internet Explorer	<ul><li>Click *Tools* or press *Alt+X*.</li><li>Click *Internet options*.</li><li>Click the *General tab*, if necessary.</li><li>Enter the URL of the desired default home page in the Home page box. If you enter URLs of several pages, each page will display in a new tab when the browser is opened.</li><li>Click *Use current* located below the Home page box if you want to use the page that is currently active. Click *Use default* for the page set during the installation of the browser, or click *Use blank* if you want the home page to be a blank tab. Click OK.</li></ul>
Safari	<ul><li>Click *Safari*.</li><li>Click *Preferences*.</li><li>Click the *General* pane.</li><li>Enter the URL of the desired home page in the home page box. Press Enter.</li><li>Alternatively, click *Set to Current Page* to make the current Web page the home page.</li><li>Close the General Preference window.</li></ul>

> **TROUBLESHOOTING:** If you notice that settings, such as the browser's home page, have changed but you didn't change them, you may have malware or a program installed on your computer. You can get malware from downloading files or visiting insecure sites. You will first need to remove the malicious program or malware from your computer to regain control of your browser.

Notify When Closing Multiple Tabs

STEP 2 ▶ Current browsers make use of tabs enabling one browser session to contain many Web pages. So the accidental closing of a current browser can result in the loss of many Web pages. To help prevent this unplanned closing, each popular browser, except Chrome, has an option provided in its initial download that, when activated, issues a warning when closing multiple tabs. Chrome requires the downloading of an add-on program to activate this option. This warning can avoid the frustration of losing hours of research. Refer to Table 1.7 for the location of the notification feature in the browser of your choice.

You might reduce annoyance from an accidental browser closing if your browser is set to view recently closed windows. This option is located under History, located under Settings in Firefox and Safari and under *View favorites, feeds, and history* icon in Internet Explorer. In Chrome, click Customize and control Google Chrome and select History from the menu. All browsing activity is listed by date and time. You can re-open pages by clicking each page listed in Chrome's history list. This feature presents an option to re-open accidentally closed Web pages, but unintentionally closing a browser that has multiple tabs open is best prevented by activating the notification feature.

TABLE 1.7	Notify When Closing Multiple Tabs
Browser	**Location of Option to Notify When Closing Multiple Tabs**
Chrome	Chrome does not contain the notification feature.
Firefox	• Click the *Open menu* button. • Click *Options*. • Click the *Tabs* panel. • *Warn me when closing multiple tabs* is the default option and should already be checked (see Figure 1.16). • Click *OK*.
Internet Explorer	• Click the *Tools* icon. • Click *Internet options*. • Click the General tab, if necessary. • Under Tabs, click *Tabs*. • *Warn me when closing multiple tabs* is the default option and should already be checked. • Click *OK*. Click *OK* again.
Safari	Safari does not contain the notification feature.

FIGURE 1.15 Google Chrome's Window Close Protector Extension

Android is a trademark of Google Inc. Use of this trademark is subject to Google Permissions.

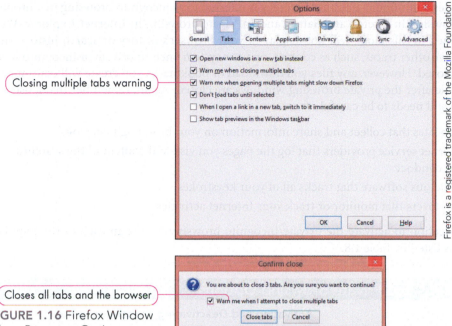

Closing multiple tabs warning

Closes all tabs and the browser

Firefox is a registered trademark of the Mozilla Foundation

FIGURE 1.16 Firefox Window Close Protector Option

Firefox is a registered trademark of the Mozilla Foundation

Manage Browsing History

STEP 3

Editing your *browser history* settings can be important, especially on systems being shared by several individuals. Most often your browsing history is useful, as it fast tracks Web surfing by giving AutoComplete suggestions. If the desired site displays in the suggested AutoComplete list, you can just click it. But browsing history may seriously compromise your privacy, as it contains details about each URL you type in the Address/Location bar. If you are sharing a system with others, they will be able to view the Web sites you visited or download the files you downloaded. To protect your privacy, on a shared computer, you should delete the browsing history.

Deleting your browsing history clears only the contents of the history file where your browser records the addresses of visited Web sites; your activities are not entirely eradicated. If you have downloaded an image from the Web, clearing your browsing history will remove the URL; however, the image will remain in the Downloads folder on your computer. Additionally, every time you access the Internet you are assigned an *IP address* by your ISP. An IP address is a unique identifying numeric code assigned to you and is associated with you for as long as you are logged on to the Internet. Every site you visit while connected to the Internet is then logged, time stamped, and associated with the IP address assigned to you for that Internet session. Erasing the browsing history file on your own computer does not erase the log kept by your ISP. Using good judgment is still the rule when browsing the Web.

Other features in the history section of most browsers enable you to recall more than just your browsing history. Firefox's History settings are located in the Privacy panel, which is opened by selecting Options from the *Menu button* commands. Some additional choices in this panel include:

- Remember search and form history. Form history is the content you type when filling out a form on a Web page.
- Clear history when Firefox closes.
- Use History and Bookmarks in the Address/Location bar AutoComplete feature.

Refer to Table 1.8 for the location of similar History settings in other browsers.

Activate Privacy (Incognito or InPrivate) Browsing

STEP 4

How do you search for a birthday gift for a family member without having the search information added to the system's browsing history? Is there any other option besides erasing the entire browsing history and upsetting the rest of the family? A mode on popular browsers that provides a minimum amount of secrecy is referred to as incognito browsing in Chrome, Private browsing in Firefox and Safari, and InPrivate browsing in Internet Explorer. Web pages opened in this mode will not display in your browser's history or search history and will not leave other traces, such as cookies, on your system once all private or incognito windows are closed. However, any files you download or bookmarks you create will continue to be accessible after the private browsing windows are closed. Again, remember that a user in this mode still needs to be careful of:

- Web sites that collect and share information on your browsing behavior
- Internet service providers that log the pages you visit and content of the searches you conduct
- Malicious software that tracks all of your keystrokes
- Employers that monitor or track your Internet activities

The location to activate the private/incognito browsing feature in each of the popular browsers is listed in Table 1.8.

TABLE 1.8 Browsing History Settings and Private Browsing Options

Browser	Location of History Settings	Activating and Deactivating Private/Incognito Browsing
Chrome	<ul><li>Click *Customize and control Google Chrome.*</li><li>Click *Settings.*</li><li>Click the *History* option on the left side of the Settings Web page.</li><li>Click the *Clear browsing data* button on the History Web page that appears. Check the options you want to activate in the window that opens and click the *Clear browsing data* button.</li></ul>	<ul><li>Click *Customize and control Google Chrome.*</li><li>Click *New incognito window* (see Figure 1.17).</li><li>A new browser session opens with a tab that contains an explanation of what going incognito means along with a blank Address/Location bar.</li><li>End the incognito session by closing the browser window.</li></ul>
Firefox	<ul><li>Click the *Menu* button.</li><li>Click *Options.*</li><li>Click the *Privacy* panel.</li><li>In the History section, choose Firefox will: Use custom settings for the history, then check the boxes of the options you want to activate.</li><li>Click *OK.*</li></ul>	<ul><li>Click the *Open menu* button.</li><li>Click the *New Private Window* button.</li><li>A new, private browsing session opens, a purple mask icon can be seen at the top-right, and the tab is labeled as Private Browsing.</li><li>End private browsing by closing the browser window.</li></ul>
Internet Explorer	<ul><li>Click the *Tools* icon.</li><li>Point to *Safety.*</li><li>Select *Delete browsing history.*</li><li>Check the box to the left of the options in the Delete Browsing History window that you want to delete from your browsing history.</li><li>Click *Delete.*</li></ul>	<ul><li>Click the *Tools* icon.</li><li>Point to *Safety.*</li><li>Click *InPrivate Browsing.*</li><li>A new, private browsing session opens with a blue tab to the left of the Address/Location bar identified by the label InPrivate.</li><li>End InPrivate browsing by closing the browser window.</li></ul>
Safari	<ul><li>Click *History* on the menu bar</li><li>Click *Clear History.*</li><li>Click *Clear.*</li></ul>	<ul><li>Click *File* on the menu bar.</li><li>Click *New Private Window.*</li><li>A new, private browsing window opens with the text Private Browsing Enabled.</li><li>End Private browsing by closing the browser window.</li></ul>

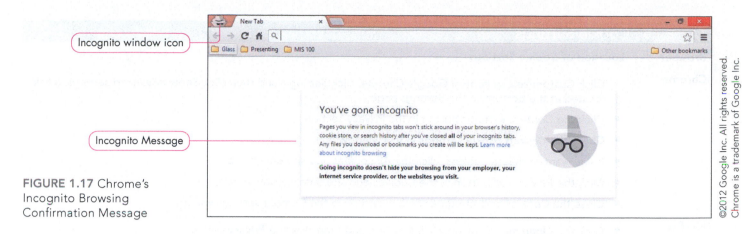

Incognito window icon

Incognito Message

FIGURE 1.17 Chrome's Incognito Browsing Confirmation Message

Restrict Cookies

STEP 5 ▶ A *cookie* is a simple text file that is saved on your computer and contains an identification number assigned to you by the site you are visiting. When you return to that site at a later date, the site opens its own cookie and uses the identification number to locate information it has stored about you on its server. This information can be used to customize your Web page's appearance or implement features such as a shopping cart. You should be familiar with two types of cookies. A *first-party cookie* is a text file generated by a Web site you requested to view. This is how Internet retailers such as Amazon make seemingly appropriate suggestions for books, video games, and electronic devices. Cookies make browsing more personalized to the user.

A *third-party cookie* is a text file generated by a Web site other than the one you requested. For example, if you enter the URL southwest.com and a cookie from southwest.com is placed on your computer, it is a first-party cookie. If flycheap.com tries to place a cookie on your computer after visiting southwest.com, that cookie would be a third-party cookie, as you are not on the www.flycheap.com Web site.

First-party cookies can actually enhance and facilitate your browsing experience, but most browsers have an option to block third-party cookies. For the location of cookie settings in each browser, refer to Table 1.9. Because the previous tables have explicitly stated the steps to locate several browser features, an abbreviated syntax will be used in Table 1.9 and all tables that follow.

Some of the usual concerns about cookies are:

- Can cookies collect personal information about you from your computer? No. Cookies are simple text files that hold an identification number usable by only the Web site that deposited that cookie on your computer. They do not contain personal information.
- Are cookies used often? Yes.
- Are cookies harmful? No. A cookie contains an identification number that is relative only to the originating Web site. Additional information about your browsing habits or site customization is stored on the server of that Web site and is only accessible by retrieving the identification number stored in its cookie saved on your computer.
- Can a virus be transmitted by a cookie? No. A cookie is just a text file.
- Can the personal information on your hard disk be read by a cookie? No. The cookie can only be re-opened by the server of the Web page that deposited it on your computer system in order to retrieve your assigned identification number.
- Can cookie files be deleted from your computer? Yes. Deleting cookies is a choice in the Options/Settings/Preferences of most browsers. Refer to Table 1.9 for the location of cookie-related options in your browser. Deleting cookies can have a down side. If you went to a Web site, such as a banking institution, and had accepted the option to remember your login name and password, deleting the cookie for that institution will require you to re-enter your username and passwords when you return to that site.

TABLE 1.9 Cookie Settings

Browser	Location of Cookie Settings
Chrome	• Click *Customize and control Google Chrome*, click *Settings*, and then click *Show advanced settings*, a link located at the bottom of the Settings page. • Click the *Content settings* button in the Privacy section. • Check the desired cookie settings in this window. • If you want to delete cookies, click the *All cookies and site data* button. • Click the *Remove all* button in the Cookies and site data window that opens. • Close the Cookies and site data window and close the Content settings window.
Firefox	• Click the *Open menu* button, click *Options*, and then click the *Privacy* panel. • Under History, Set Firefox will: to *Use custom settings for history*. • If you want to delete cookies, click the *Show Cookies* button on the right side of the Options dialog box. • When the Cookies dialog box opens, you have two options. You can select individual cookies and click the *Remove Cookie* button. This option might be hard, as the file name of a cookie and its related Web site might not be the same. Your other choice is to just click the *Remove All Cookies* button and delete all cookies saved on your system. • Click *Close* in the Cookies dialog box. • Click *OK* in the Options dialog box.
Internet Explorer	• Click the *Tools* icon, click *Internet options*, and then click the *Privacy* tab. • Adjust the slider bar in the Settings section. The options on the slider include Block All Cookies, High, Medium High, Medium, Low, and Accept All Cookies. An explanation for the actions performed by each option appears as you move the slider. • If you want to delete cookies, click the *General* tab. • Click the *Delete* button in the Browsing history section. • Select the *Cookies and website data* box in the Delete Browsing History dialog box that opens. • Click *Delete*. • Click *OK* in the *Internet Options* window.
Safari	• Click *Safari* on the menu bar, click *Preferences*, and then click the *Privacy* pane. • In the Privacy pane, you can choose to Block cookies From third parties and advertisers, Block cookies Always, or Block cookies Never. • If you want to delete all cookies, click the *Remove all website data* button in the Privacy pane. • Click the *Remove Now* button in the window that opens. • If you want to delete specific cookies, click the Details button in the Privacy pane. Select the individual cookie(s) and click Remove. • Close the Privacy Preference window.

Quick Concepts

1. What is the purpose of a homepage? *(p. 17)*

2. What is browsing history? Why might someone want to clear their browsing history? *(p. 21)*

3. What is the purpose of incognito or InPrivate browsing? *(p. 21)*

4. What is the difference between first-party cookies and third-party cookies? Are all cookies bad? *(p. 23)*

Hands-On Exercises

2 Personalize Your Browser

After familiarizing yourself with common browser features, you are ready to personalize your computer by changing some of the Internet Explorer browser settings to suit your browsing habits.

Skills covered: Set a Home Page • Notify When Closing Multiple Tabs • Manage Browsing History • Activate Private (incognito or InPrivate) Browsing • Restrict Cookies

STEP 1 ›› SET A HOME PAGE

The Web site for FactorX is not quite finished. In the meantime, you want to set a home page that is appropriate. You decide on www.nasa.gov, as it is a government-sponsored site. Refer to Figure 1.18 as you complete Step 1. If a browser other than Internet Explorer is used for this exercise, your results will not be the same as those displayed.

Step d: Enter www.nasa.gov in address bar

Step e: Click Tools icon, click Internet options

Step f: Click Use current

FIGURE 1.18 Open www.nasa.gov and Make It Your Home Page

a. Start Word. At the top of a blank document, type **Hands-on Exercise 2** and press Enter. On the next line, type *your full name* and the *date*.

b. Save the document as **wbr01h2_LastFirst.docx** and minimize the window.

c. Open **Internet Explorer** and verify that only one tab is opened. If multiple tabs appear, close all but one.

d. Type **www.nasa.gov** in the **Address/Location bar** and press **Enter**.

e. Click **Internet options** from the Tools menu. The General tab should be displayed.

f. Click **Use current** in the Home page section. Because you only have one tab open and the www.nasa.gov page displayed, clicking **Use current** will automatically enter its URL into the Home page box.

g. Click **Snipping Tool** in the Accessories folder of the Start menu. You will create a snip of your browser's window.

h. Click the **New snip arrow** and click **Full-screen Snip**.

i. Click **File** on the menu bar located in the Snipping Tool window that opens and click **Save As** from the list of File options.

j. Select the drive and folder in the Save As dialog box in which you want to save your image and name the snip **wbr01h2snip1_LastFirst.jpg**.

k. Save and close the JPEG file.

l. Select the Word document **wbr01h2_LastFirst.docx** to make it active.

m. Move the cursor to the end of the Word document, press **Enter**, and then select **Pictures** on the Insert tab.

n. Navigate to the *wbr01h2snip1_LastFirst.jpg* file and click **Insert**.

o. Click **File** and click **Save**. Minimize the window and keep the file open.

p. Click **Cancel** in the **Internet Options window**.

STEP 2 ›› NOTIFY WHEN CLOSING MULTIPLE TABS

You will be comparing the Web sites, marketing strategies, and products of your competitors and suppliers. In order to prevent retracing steps and wasting time, you want to be sure that the feature to notify when closing multiple tabs is in effect. Refer to Figure 1.19 as you complete Step 2.

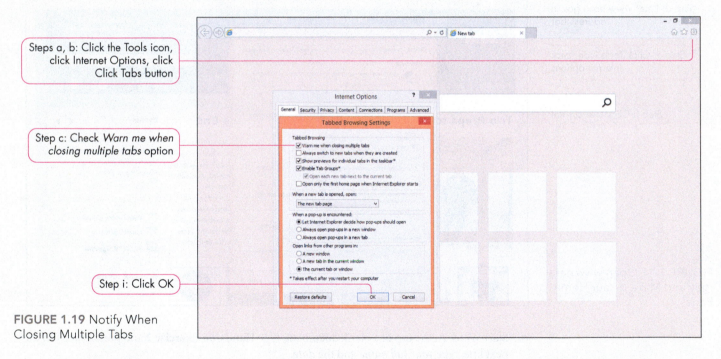

FIGURE 1.19 Notify When Closing Multiple Tabs

a. Click the **Tools icon** and click **Internet options**. The General tab should be displayed.

b. Click the **Tabs** button in the Tabs section of the General tab.

c. Make sure a check mark appears to the left of the *Warn me when closing multiple tabs* option.

d. Use the Snipping Tool to save a JPEG snip of this window as **wbr01h2snip2_LastFirst.jpg**.

e. Make the Word document **wbr01h2_LastFirst.docx** active.

f. Move the cursor to the end of the Word document, press **Enter**, click the **Insert tab,** and then click **Pictures**.

g. Select the *wbr01h2snip2_LastFirst.jpg* file and click **Insert**.

h. Save the *wbr01h2_LastFirst.docx* file. Minimize the window, keeping the file open.

i. Click **OK** in the Internet Explorer Tabbed Browsing Settings dialog box.

j. Click **OK** in the Internet Options window.

STEP 3 ▶▶ MANAGE BROWSING HISTORY

You are the only user of your computer. You like the AutoComplete feature of the One Box of Internet Explorer and want to check your browser settings to make sure that the browser's history will not be erased when the browser closes. Refer to Figure 1.20 as you complete Step 3.

Steps a, b: Click the Tools icon, point to Safety, click Delete browsing history

Step c: Ensure only first two options are selected

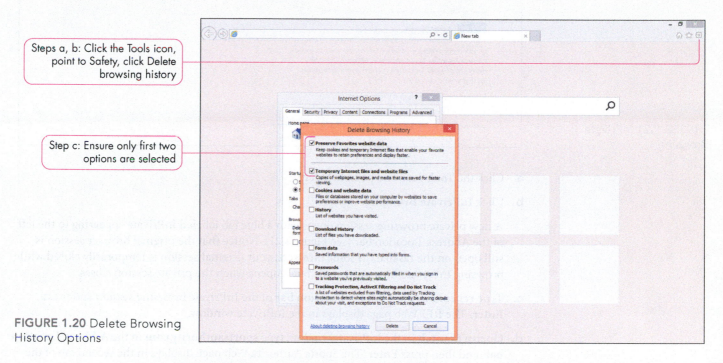

FIGURE 1.20 Delete Browsing History Options

a. Click the **Tools icon** and point to **Safety**.

b. Click **Delete browsing history**.

c. Make sure only the first two options, Preserve Favorites website data and Temporary Internet files and website files, in the Delete Browsing History dialog box are selected. If other options are checked, uncheck them. This will preserve your browsing history and not delete your cookies.

d. Use the Snipping Tool to save the JPEG snip of this dialog box as **wbr01h2snip3_LastFirst.jpg**.

e. Select the Word document *wbr01h2_LastFirst.docx*.

f. Move the cursor to the end of the Word document, press **Enter**, click the **Insert tab,** and then click **Pictures**.

g. Select the **wbr01h2snip3_LastFirst.jpg** file and click **Insert**.

h. Save the **wbr01h2_LastFirst.docx** file. Minimize the window and keep the file open.

i. Click **Delete** in the Delete Browsing History dialog box of Internet Explorer to actually delete the content of the items checked.

At times, you may not want Web sites to display in your AutoComplete suggestion list. You have heard of InPrivate browsing and want to try a session to see how it works. Refer to Figures 1.21 and 1.22 as you complete Step 4.

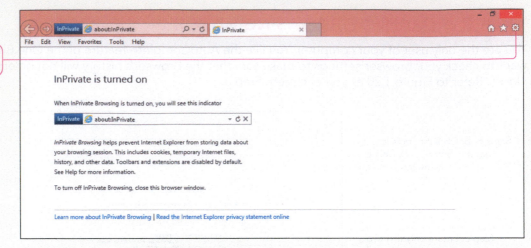

Steps a, b: Click Tools icon, Point to Safety, click InPrivate Browsing

FIGURE 1.21 InPrivate Browsing

a. Click the **Tools icon** and point to **Safety**.

b. Click **InPrivate Browsing**.

A new private browsing session opens with a blue tab labeled InPrivate appearing to the left of the Address/Location bar (see Figure 1.21). Notice that the original browser session is still open on the taskbar. In some browsers, your original session is temporarily closed while browsing InPrivate/incognito mode but reopens when the private session closes.

c. Type **rei.com** in the **Address/Location bar** of the InPrivate browsing session and press **Enter**. The REI Web page displays in the InPrivate window.

d. Open a **new tab** in the InPrivate window, type **sportsauthority.com** in the **Address/Location bar**, and then press **Enter**. The Sports Authority Web page displays in the second tab of the InPrivate window.

e. Use the Snipping Tool to save the JPEG snip of the InPrivate window as **wbr01h2snip4_LastFirst.jpg**.

f. Select the Word document *wbr01h2_LastFirst.docx*.

g. Move the cursor to the end of the document, press **Enter**, click the **Insert tab**, and then click **Pictures**.

h. Locate the *wbr01h2snip4_LastFirst.jpg* file and click **Insert**.

i. Save the *wbr01h2_LastFirst.docx* file. **Minimize** the window, keeping the file open.

j. Click the **Close (X) button** in the top-right corner of the Internet Explorer InPrivate window to close the InPrivate Browsing window.

k. Click **Close all tabs** in the window that opens.

l. Internet Explorer should appear on your desktop. Verify that the browser window does not have the InPrivate blue tab in front of the Address/Location bar.

m. Type **sports** in the **Address/Location bar**. The site www.sportsauthority.com should not display in the AutoComplete list of suggestions (see Figure 1.22). Try entering **rei** in the **Address/Location bar**; again, www.rei.com should not display in the AutoComplete list of suggestions. This validates that the Web pages viewed in the InPrivate browsing session are not stored in the browsing history and are therefore not available in the AutoComplete feature in a not InPrivate session.

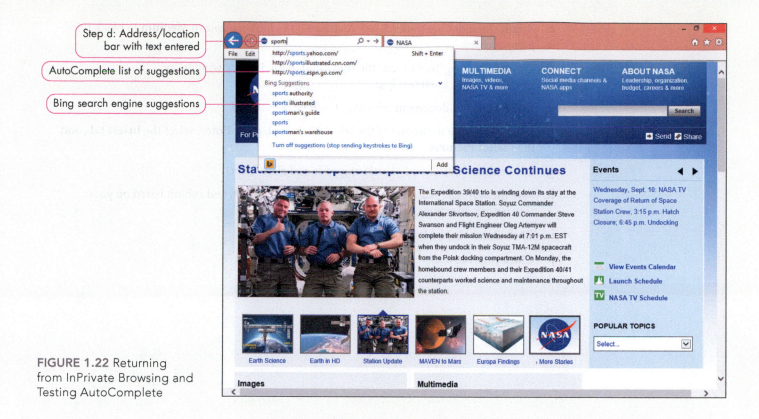

Step d: Address/location bar with text entered

AutoComplete list of suggestions

Bing search engine suggestions

FIGURE 1.22 Returning from InPrivate Browsing and Testing AutoComplete

TROUBLESHOOTING: If the URL of either Web site does appear in the AutoComplete list of suggestions, you must have visited that Web site in a not InPrivate session prior to doing this Hands-On Exercise.

STEP 5 ▶ RESTRICT COOKIES

You do not want to be bothered during the workday with ads from Web sites that you have not visited. You know that cookies, in general, enhance a browsing experience by making it more personal. But after doing some research, you realize that you can block third-party cookies and alleviate some irritating, unsolicited ads. Refer to Figure 1.23 as you complete Step 5.

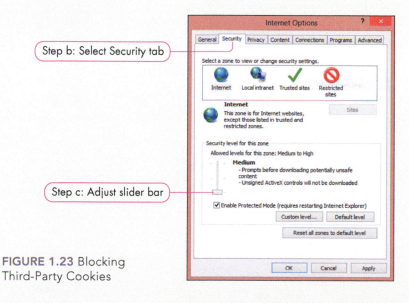

Step b: Select Security tab

Step c: Adjust slider bar

FIGURE 1.23 Blocking Third-Party Cookies

a. Click the **Tools icon** and click **Internet options**.

b. Select the **Privacy tab**.

c. Adjust the slider bar under *Select a setting for the Internet zone* to **Medium** to block third-party cookies.

d. Use the Snipping Tool to save the JPEG snip of the Privacy window as **wbr01h2snip5_LastFirst.jpg**.

e. Make the Word document *wbr01h2_LastFirst.docx* active.

f. Move the cursor to the end of the Word document, press **Enter**, select the **Insert tab**, and then select **Pictures**.

g. Locate the *wbr01h2snip5_LastFirst.jpg* file and click **Insert**.

h. Save the *wbr01h2_LastFirst.docx* file, close the document, and submit based on your instructor's directions.

i. Click **Cancel** in the Internet Explorer Privacy window.

j. **Close** your browser.

Accelerate Browsing

In addition to changing settings to personalize your browsing experience, you can expedite Web research by marking Web pages that you might want to re-visit. This feature prevents you from sifting through search results to relocate a reference used previously.

In this section, you will learn to mark, view, access, manage, rename, and delete a Web page you want to frequently re-visit. You also will learn which browsers permit a Web page to be tagged and pinned and how to perform these actions.

Becoming Familiar with the Favorites or Bookmarks Feature

One of the primary uses of a browser is to save time by quickly being able to return to a Web site or Web page you found in an earlier browsing session. *Favorites* or *bookmarks* (the name varies depending on the browser) are a collection of Web pages or folders that contain related bookmarked Web pages. The use of this browser feature enables you to set sites you visit frequently or deem important in an easy-to-access area that re-opens the site with just a click of the mouse.

Make a Favorite or Bookmark

STEP 1 ▷ Most browsers have an icon that, when clicked, automatically adds the Web page that you are viewing to your browser's favorites or bookmarks list. Refer to Table 1.10 to locate the icon used to insert the current Web page into your favorite/bookmark list, and the location of that icon in your browser's window. Three of the four popular browsers will open a dialog box when the favorites/bookmarks icon is clicked that enables you to name the Web page you are designating as a favorite or bookmark. The exception is Firefox, which automatically names the bookmark; simply re-clicking the icon will open the Edit This Bookmark dialog box that contains an option to rename the bookmark.

TABLE 1.10 Favorites or Bookmarks Icon		
Browser	**Favorites/Bookmarks Icon**	**Icon Location**
Chrome	Star icon	Right side of the Omnibox.
Firefox	Star icon	Right side of the Awesome Bar.
Internet Explorer	Star icon	Right side of the browser's window to the left of Tools. Click the *Add to favorites* button from the menu that displays.
Safari	Plus sign	Left side of the Address/Location bar. (Depending on the version of Safari, this button may only appear when the mouse is placed over this area on the screen.)

View the Favorites or Bookmarks Bar

STEP 2 ▷ Typically, there are a few ways to view and access the Web pages you have designated as favorites or bookmarks. Most browsers enable you to display the *favorites/bookmarks bar* at the top of the browser's window. Refer to Table 1.11 to learn how to display favorites/bookmarks in each of the popular browsers. Additionally, Figure 1.24 shows how this bar displays in each of the four popular browsers.

Items that display on the favorites/bookmarks bar include individual Web pages you have marked as a favorite or bookmark, folders that represent categories into which you have organized some of your favorite/bookmarked Web pages, and browser-specific options such as:

- Most Visited and Getting Started in Firefox
- Suggested Sites in Internet Explorer
- Show Top Sites and Show Reading List in Safari

Figure 1.24 displays the familiar yellow folder on three of the browser's bars; Safari, however, indicates its folders by displaying the folder name followed by an arrow that, when clicked, displays a menu of bookmarked pages within that folder from which you can select.

> **TROUBLESHOOTING:** Your browser's favorites/bookmarks bar may display differently than what is shown in Figure 1.24. Your favorites/bookmarks Web pages and folders will most definitely be different than those displayed. But even the browser-specific options listed above might not display. That is because some of the browser's options can be deleted by right-clicking on them and selecting Delete from the shortcut menu. The exception is the Show Top Sites and Show Reading List in Safari; these browser options cannot be deleted from the Bookmarks Bar.

TABLE 1.11 Making the Favorites or Bookmarks Bar Visible

Browser	Making the Favorites/Bookmarks Bar Visible
Chrome	Click *Customize and control Google Chrome*, point to *Bookmarks*, and then click *Show bookmarks bar*.
Firefox	Click *Show your bookmarks* in the top-right corner of the browser's window (an icon to the right of the star that resembles a list of items), select *Bookmarks Toolbar* from the list, click *View Bookmarks Toolbar*.
Internet Explorer	Right-click the title bar to display the shortcut menu and click *Favorites bar*.
Safari	Click *Bookmark* icon to view Bookmark Sidebar. If the Bookmarks Sidebar is already visible, click *Bookmark* icon to hide the sidebar.

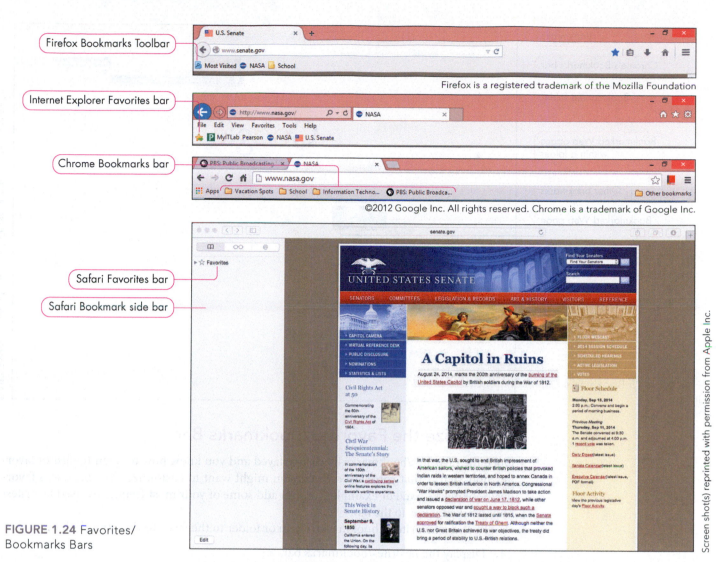

Labels pointing to the figure (left side, top to bottom):
- Firefox Bookmarks Toolbar
- Internet Explorer Favorites bar
- Chrome Bookmarks bar
- Safari Favorites bar
- Safari Bookmark side bar

Firefox is a registered trademark of the Mozilla Foundation

©2012 Google Inc. All rights reserved. Chrome is a trademark of Google Inc.

Screen shot(s) reprinted with permission from Apple Inc.

FIGURE 1.24 Favorites/Bookmarks Bars

Locate and Open a Favorite or Bookmarked Web Page

Once you have marked a Web page as a favorite or bookmark and displayed the favorites/bookmarks bar, how do you re-open a Web page you previously marked as a favorite or bookmark? Re-opening a Web page that you have marked as a favorite or bookmark within your browser can usually be done by clicking a button. The description of the favorite/bookmark option/icon and its location for several browsers are listed in Table 1.12. When the appropriate item is clicked in each browser, a list of the Web pages you marked as a favorite/bookmark is displayed in the current browser.

Follow the steps below to view bookmarked Web pages or folders in Chrome as shown in Figure 1.25.

TABLE 1.12   View List of Favorites or Bookmarks Buttons

Browser	Favorites/Bookmarks Icon	Location of Option/Icon
Chrome	⭐	Right side of the Bookmarks bar.
Firefox	⭐ 📋	Right side of the Bookmark this page (Star) Icon.
Internet Explorer	🏠 ⭐ ⚙	Right side of the tabs row to the left of the Tools icon.
Safari	📖 ▦	Left side of the Bookmarks Bar.

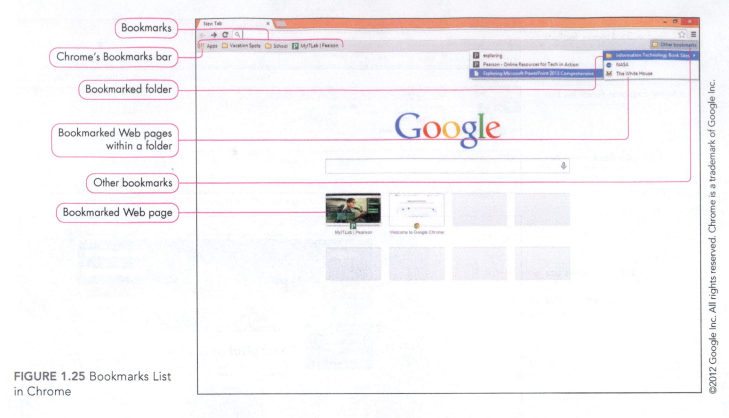

FIGURE 1.25 Bookmarks List in Chrome

Customize the Favorites/Bookmarks Bar

Once the favorites/bookmarks bar is displayed and you know how to open the list of favorites/bookmarks that you have created, you might want to customize your browser's favorites/bookmarks bar. For example, you can add some of your most frequently used favorites/bookmarked items to the bar.

To add a favorite or bookmarked item or folder to the favorites/bookmarks bar:

1. Display the favorites/bookmarks bar.
2. View the favorites/bookmarks list.
3. From the list, drag the desired favorite/bookmark to the favorites/bookmarks bar. When you see an insertion indicator, release the mouse and drop the item on the bar.

You can position a bookmark on the favorites/bookmarks bar when it is created. In Chrome and Firefox, click, or re-click, the Bookmark this page icon (a star in Chrome and Firefox). A window opens containing a folder option in Chrome. Select the Bookmarks bar from the options displayed. In Firefox, click the Show your bookmarks icon and drag the bookmark to the bar. In Safari, click and hold the plus sign, choose the location for the bookmark from the list of options. A checkmark briefly appears after the bookmark has been added to the chosen location. In Internet Explorer, click the View Favorites, Feeds, and History icon. Click the arrow to the right of the Add to favorites button from the menu that is displayed. Click the Add to Favorites bar from the options displayed.

> **TROUBLESHOOTING:** You can drag a link from a Web page opened in any browser directly to the favorites/bookmarks bar of that browser. The bookmark is for the link location, not the Web page that the link appeared in.

A bookmark can be deleted from the favorites/bookmarks bar by right-clicking the bookmark and selecting Delete from the shortcut menu. Notice that this not only deletes the bookmark from the bar but also from the favorites/bookmarks list. If you want to remove the bookmark from the favorites/bookmarks bar but keep it in the favorites/bookmarks list in Firefox, drag the bookmark from the bar to the Bookmark button that is used to view the Bookmarks list or drag it to the Other Bookmarks folder in Chrome. Open the Bookmarks list; the bookmark will be displayed in the list. If you want to reposition it within the list, drag it up or down to a new location in the list. In Internet Explorer and Safari, you first need to display the Favorites list or Show all bookmarks list. In Internet Explorer, click Favorites in the displayed list. In Safari, click Bookmarks sidebar icon. Drag the bookmark that you want to remove from the Bookmarks sidebar to the position in the Bookmarks list where you want it to be inserted.

Managing Favorites or Bookmarks

The favorites/bookmarks list can get out of control with regard to both length and layout. When a site is marked as a favorite/bookmark, depending on the browser, it usually is placed at the bottom of the favorites/bookmarks list. However, when you organize your bookmarked Web pages into folders, you will be able to locate, access, and open relevant Web pages quicker.

Organize Your Favorites or Bookmarks

STEP 3 > The most common organizational methods used in filing systems are alphabetical order and grouping by content. The same is true for your favorites/bookmarks list. Alphabetically ordering items in this list is easily accomplished by dragging the bookmarks in the correct alphabetical position. Grouping takes a few extra steps and requires you to make folders in the favorites/bookmarks list. Once folders are created and labeled, you simply drag related items into their appropriate folder. Folders can also be alphabetized by dragging them into the correct alphabetical order. Refer to Table 1.13 to create a folder in the favorites/bookmarks list in any of the four popular browsers.

Browser	Making a Folder in the Favorites/Bookmarks List
TABLE 1.13	**Making a Folder in the Favorites/Bookmarks List**
Chrome	• Display the Bookmarks bar if it is not visible. • Right-click the *Other bookmarks* icon and click *Add folder*. • Type the name of the folder in the Name box of the New folder window. • Click *Save*.
Firefox	• Display the *Bookmarks Toolbar* if it is not visible. • Right-click the *Show All Bookmarks* option in the menu displayed and click *New Folder* from the shortcut menu. • Type the name of the folder in the Name box of the New Folder dialog box. • Click *Add*.
Internet Explorer	• Click the *View favorites, feeds, and history* icon, located on the right side of the tabs row. • Click the *arrow* to the right of the *Add to favorites*. • Click *Organize favorites* from the list of options displayed. • Click the *New Folder* button in the *Organize Favorites dialog box*. • Type the name of the folder in the box. • Press *Enter*. • Click *Close*.
Safari	• Display the Bookmarks sidebar if it is not visible. • Click *Bookmarks* in the menu bar. • Click *Add Bookmark Folder*. • Type the name of the folder in the untitled folder box. • Press *Enter*.

> **TROUBLESHOOTING:** When creating folders using the steps in Table 1.13, your new folder will be in the main favorites/bookmarks list. If right-clicking within the favorites/bookmarks list of any browser and using the New Folder or Add Folder option from the shortcut menu, you need to be careful. Where you place the pointer when you right-click determines where the new folder will be positioned. If you right-click just a bookmark in the main favorites/bookmarks list, the newly created folder will be viewable on the main list. If, however, you right-click an existing folder, the newly created folder will be a subfolder of the existing folder and not visible on the main list. A misplaced folder can easily be repositioned by dragging the folder to its desired location.

Rename a Favorite or Bookmark Page or Folder

At times, you may want to identify a favorite or bookmark by a name or feature that is important to your research. Frequently, the original name of the saved Web site is inapplicable as your research progresses and becomes more specific. Favorite or bookmarked Web pages and folders in the favorites/bookmarks list can be renamed. Chrome is used in the steps below; however, this action can be performed in a similar way in every browser.

1. Display your list of favorites or bookmarks.
2. Right-click the Web page or folder name in the list that you want to change.
3. Select Rename for a folder and Edit for a Web page.
4. Type a new name.
5. Press Enter or click Save.

Delete a Favorite or Bookmark

STEP 5 > Deleting pages and folders in a favorites/bookmarks list that are no longer needed is a good practice and keeps the list uncluttered and organized. Deleting a favorite/bookmark is accomplished by right-clicking the bookmark in the favorites/bookmarks bar or in the favorites/bookmarks list and choosing Delete from the shortcut menu displayed.

Exploring Browser-Specific Accelerators

Browsers have several similar features so a user can easily alternate between them. However, some browsers have unique features that are not mimicked in others and may make your session in that browser more convenient, your sites and search results presented more rapidly, and your overall browsing experience more efficient. Some of these unique features are described below.

Tagging a Web Page in Firefox

STEP 6 > Firefox lets you add a tag to a bookmark, a feature that is unique only to Firefox. A *tag* is one or more key terms that will then become associated with a bookmark. The purpose of tags is to provide additional assistance to the AutoComplete feature so that its list of options is more relative to your usage and sites that you have bookmarked. For example, assume you had tagged several bookmarked Web sites with the key term *medical*. By typing *medical* in the Address/Location bar, any URL in your history with the word *medical* in it would appear in the AutoComplete list, but so would any bookmarks that have *medical* as a tag.

To add a tag to a bookmark in Firefox:

1. Click the bookmark and open the Web page in the browser's window.
2. Click the Edit this bookmark icon to open the Edit This Bookmark window (see Figure 1.26). Three boxes appear in this window:

   - The Name box where you enter a new identifying name for the bookmark.
   - The Folder list that enables you to select an existing folder in which to place the bookmark. Or, select the Folder arrow, click Choose, and then click New Folder to create a new folder.
   - The Tags box where you enter a tag associated with the bookmarked page. Several tags can be typed by inserting a comma between tags.

3. Click Done to save the changes and associate them with that bookmark.

Firefox Bookmark
this page icon

Enter tags separated
by commas

FIGURE 1.26 Creating Tags in Firefox

Often as research progresses, it becomes necessary to change the tags associated with a bookmark. In Firefox, this entails deleting unwanted tags and adding more relevant ones. To delete or add new tags:

1. Open the bookmarked page you want to edit.
2. Click the Edit this bookmark icon. The Edit This Bookmark window will open.
3. Add or delete tags by editing the entries in the Tags box, or click the Tags arrow to add or remove check marks for existing tags (see Figure 1.26).

Tags for a bookmark can also be edited in the Library window:

1. Click the Bookmarks button on the right side of the Bookmarks Toolbar.
2. Select Show All Bookmarks. The Library window is displayed.
3. Locate the folder that contains your bookmark or select the Bookmarks Toolbar on the left pane of the Library window, if your bookmark appears on the Bookmarks Toolbar.
4. Click the bookmark you want to edit in the right pane of the Library window.
5. Change the name, location, or tags for that bookmark by typing in the boxes at the bottom of the Library window (see Figure 1.27).
6. When all changes are complete, close the Library window, by clicking the Close (X) button located in the top-right corner.

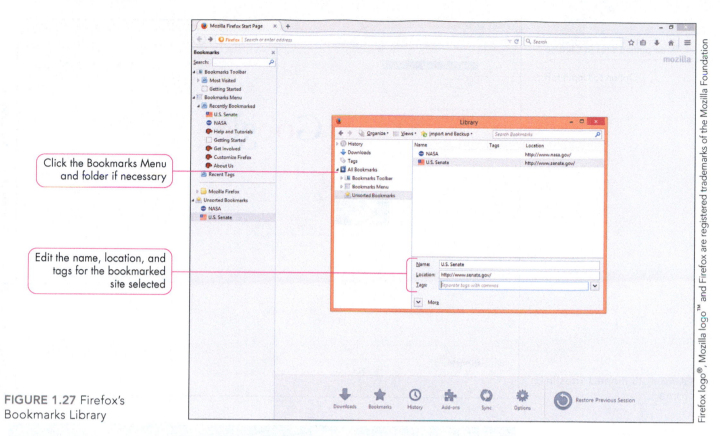

Click the Bookmarks Menu and folder if necessary

Edit the name, location, and tags for the bookmarked site selected

FIGURE 1.27 Firefox's Bookmarks Library

Pin a Web Page

STEP 7 You may have never actually thought about it, but there are many Web sites today that we treat more like programs. Gmail, Facebook, and Twitter are such sites; they update automatically and notify you when a change occurs.

Firefox, Chrome, and Internet Explorer have a solution to keeping such dynamic sites at your fingertips. It is referred to as pinning the page, site, or tab. A site is *pinned* when it is anchored on the left side of the tab row in Firefox and Chrome (see Figure 1.28). In Firefox, a *pinned tab* is referred to as an *App tab* and has the ability to take on a glow effect when the Web site has changed. This effect would happen when you receive e-mail to your pinned e-mail account or a notification to your pinned Facebook account. The glow effect enables you to visually identify the update and respond. In Internet Explorer, Web pages, Web sites, or tabs are not pinned to the tab row but can be pinned to the taskbar or pinned to the start screen in the Modern view. If a site can be pinned, it can also be unpinned. Refer to Table 1.14 for how this feature is named in each browser and steps on how to pin and unpin a site. After a site is pinned, pinned tabs can be rearranged by simply dragging them to a new location in the pinned group or, in the case of Internet Explorer, to a new location on the taskbar. The main benefit of pinning a site to the taskbar in Internet Explorer, instead of to the left of the tabs, is that a site pinned on the taskbar can be re-visited directly by clicking the site on the taskbar without having to open Internet Explorer first. Pinning a site in this way places the focus on the site, not the browser.

How does a pinned tab in Chrome and an App tab in Firefox differ from other tabs within those browsers?

- Both tabs are smaller than regular tabs and show the site icon, not the site's name. If you hover over a pinned tab, the name of the site displays.
- They do not have a Close button but can be closed by right-clicking the tab and clicking the Close option.
- When you click a hyperlink in a pinned Web page, the page displayed by the link opens in a new unpinned tab.
- When a new browser session is opened, the pinned or App tabs automatically open.
- In Firefox, when the content of an App tab changes, the site name on the tab takes on the glow effect to visually notify the user of the change.

Firefox logo®, Mozilla logo™ and Firefox are registered trademarks of the Mozilla Foundation

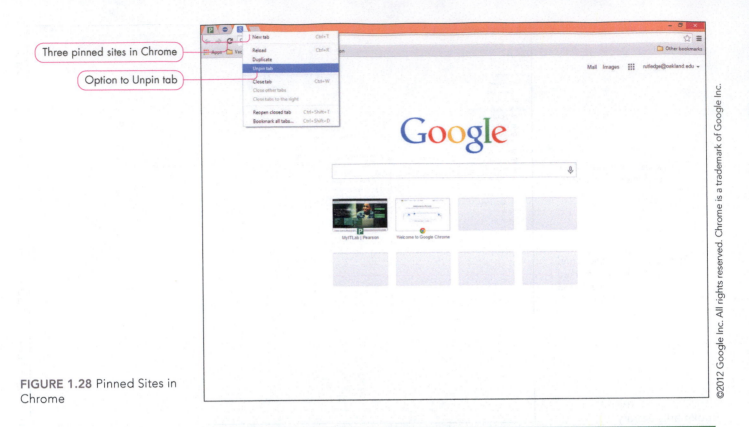

Three pinned sites in Chrome

Option to Unpin tab

FIGURE 1.28 Pinned Sites in Chrome

TABLE 1.14	Pinning a Site		
Browser	**Feature**	**Pinning a Site**	**Unpinning a Site**
Chrome	Pin tab	• Right-click the tab of the Web site. • Click *Pin tab*.	• Right-click the tab of the pinned Web site. • Click *Unpin tab*.
Firefox	App tab	• Right-click the tab of the Web site. • Click *Pin Tab*.	• Right-click the tab of the Pinned Web site. • Click *Unpin Tab*.
Internet Explorer with Windows 8	Pin a site	• Click the icon to the left of the URL, the tab of the Web site, or the Web pages icon on the New Tab page. • Drag it to the Windows 8 taskbar.	• Right-click the Web page icon on the Windows 8 taskbar. • Select *Unpin this program from taskbar*.
Safari	Feature not available		

Quick Concepts ✓

1. What is the purpose of making a bookmark or favorite? *(p. 31)*

2. What is the difference between a bookmarks bar and bookmarks list? *(p. 31)*

3. What is the purpose of pinning a Web page? *(p. 39)*

Hands-On Exercises

3 Accelerate Browsing

You like Firefox's bookmark features and decide to use this browser on your notebook. You want to set up an organized bookmark library with appropriate folders and tags so that the AutoComplete feature of the Awesome Bar will provide you with appropriate suggestions and speed up your research and comparative analysis of products, statistics, and events.

Skills covered: Make a Bookmark • View and Edit the Bookmarks Toolbar • Organize Bookmarks • Rename a Bookmark or Folder • Delete a Bookmark • Add Tags to a Bookmark • Create and Reposition App Tabs (Pinned Tabs)

STEP 1 ≫ MAKE A BOOKMARK

Your client at FactorX seems to have room for growth in the area of online sales. You want to research, locate, and bookmark several government Web sites that provide statistics on retail sales over the last few years as well as projections for future sales. Refer to Figure 1.29 as you complete Step 1. If a browser other than Firefox is used for this exercise, your results will not be the same as those displayed. The folders and bookmarks in your browser's Bookmarks list and the ones in Figure 1.29 will not be identical except for the three entered in this step.

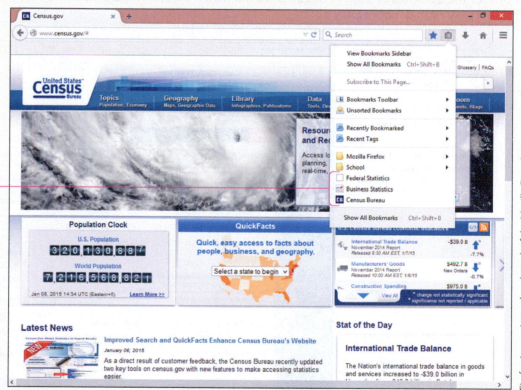

FIGURE 1.29 Three New Bookmarks

a. Start Word. At the top of a blank document, type **Hands-On Exercise 3** and press Enter. On the next line, type *your full name* and the *date*.

b. Save this document as **wbr01h3_LastFirst.docx**. You will use it later in this exercise to insert snips taken of your screen. **Minimize** the Word window.

c. Open the Firefox browser and maximize the window.

d. Type **fedstats.sites.usa.gov** in the Awesome Bar and press **Enter**. The page will automatically be redirected to fedstats.sites.usa.gov.

e. Click **Bookmark this page**.

f. Click the **Edit this bookmark icon** to open the Edit This Bookmark window.

g. Highlight the current text in the Name box (if not already highlighted), type **Federal Statistics**, click the **Folder arrow**, and then select **Bookmarks Menu**.

h. Click **Done**.

i. Repeat Steps a through h for both URLs listed below using the bookmark name provided to the right of each URL.

URL	Bookmark Name
http://www.census.gov	Census Bureau
http://www.usa.gov/Business/Business-Data.shtml	Business Statistics

> **TROUBLESHOOTING:** When you type URLs into the Address/Location bar or Awesome Bar, capital letters, hyphens, and underscores can make a difference. In the URL usa.gov /Business/Business-Data.shtml, the letters need to be capitalized as indicated and the hyphen included for the page to be located and displayed.

STEP 2 ❯❯ VIEW AND EDIT THE BOOKMARKS TOOLBAR

You want to access your bookmarked pages more quickly by displaying the Bookmarks Toolbar in your browser and adding a few of your bookmarked pages to the Bookmarks Toolbar. Refer to Figure 1.30 as you complete Step 2. The icons for the bookmarks used in this step should match those in Figure 1.30. The rest of the items on the Bookmarks Toolbar may or may not display.

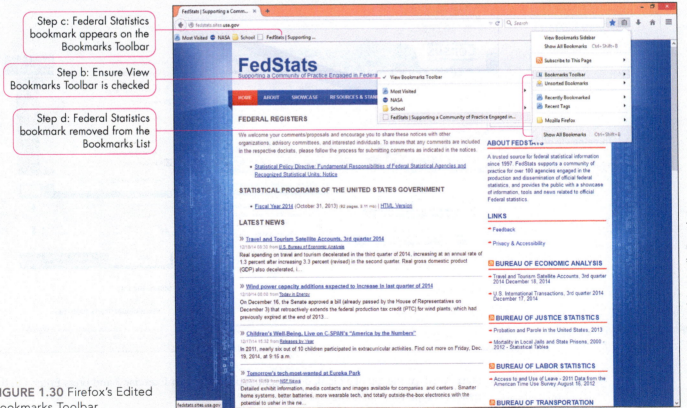

FIGURE 1.30 Firefox's Edited Bookmarks Toolbar

Firefox is a trademark of the Mozilla Foundation

a. Click **Show your bookmarks** in Firefox. This will open the bookmarks list.

b. Point to **Bookmarks Toolbar** in the menu displayed. If a check mark already appears to the left of View Bookmarks Toolbar on the menu, then do not click this option, if no check mark appears click View Bookmarks Toolbar. The Bookmarks Toolbar will display below the Address/Location bar.

c. In the list of bookmarks, locate the Federal Statistics bookmark.

d. Drag the bookmark Federal Statistics from the list to the Bookmarks Toolbar. This bookmark was moved from the Bookmarks list and now displays as an icon on the Bookmarks Toolbar.

e. Click **Federal Statistics** on the Bookmarks Toolbar; the associated Web page displays in the browser window.

STEP 3 >> ORGANIZE BOOKMARKS

After a few days of researching competitors, government information, and statistics about online sales, you realize that as your research progresses your bookmarks list will get long and unorganized. You want to create folders and move related bookmarks into a common folder. All folders need to be alphabetized. Refer to Figure 1.31 as you complete Step 3. The folders and bookmarks in your browser's bookmarks list and the ones in Figure 1.31 will not be identical except for the items created and used in this exercise.

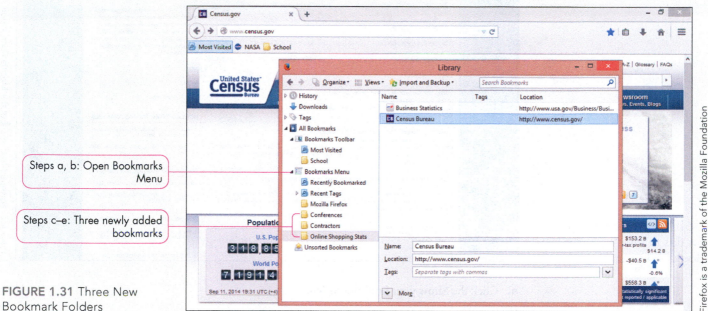

Steps a, b: Open Bookmarks Menu

Steps c–e: Three newly added bookmarks

FIGURE 1.31 Three New Bookmark Folders

Firefox is a trademark of the Mozilla Foundation

a. Click the **Show your bookmarks icon**. Click **Show All Bookmarks** in the menu displayed.

b. Right-click the **Bookmarks Menu** in the left-hand pane, and then select **New Folder** from the shortcut menu.

c. Type **Online Shopping Stats** in the **Name box** in the New Folder dialog box and click **Add**.

d. Repeat Steps b and c and create two more folders in the Bookmarks list. Name one folder **Conferences** and the other folder **Contractors**. Drag these three folders so that they are arranged in alphabetical order.

e. Click **Recently Bookmarked**. Drag the bookmarks named **Business Statistics** and **Census Bureau** into the Online Shopping Stats folder.

f. Click the Online Shopping Stats folder and confirm that both Web sites display in the folder.

STEP 4 ➤➤ RENAME A BOOKMARK OR FOLDER

After using your edited Bookmarks list for several days, you realize that some bookmarks and folders could have more meaningful names. You decide to rename a few so they are easier to identify. Refer to Figure 1.32 as you complete Step 4. The folders and bookmarks in your browser's Bookmarks list and the ones in Figure 1.32 will not be identical except for the items created and used in this exercise.

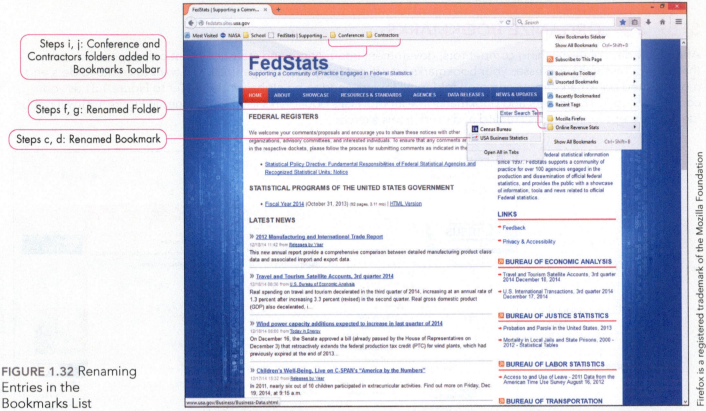

FIGURE 1.32 Renaming Entries in the Bookmarks List

a. Click the **Show your bookmarks icon**.

b. Point to **Online Shopping Stats** folder to display its contents.

c. Right-click the **Business Statistics bookmark** in the Online Shopping Stats folder and click **Properties**.

d. Enter **USA** before *Business Statistics* in the **Name box**. This makes the name of the bookmark *USA Business Statistics*.

e. Click **Save**.

f. Click the **Show your bookmarks icon**. Right-click the **Online Shopping Stats folder** in the **Bookmarks list** and click **Properties**.

g. Change *Shopping* in the Folder Name box of the Properties dialog box to **Revenue**. This makes the name of the bookmark folder *Online Revenue Stats*.

h. Click **Save**.

i. Drag the bookmark **Conferences folder** from the Bookmarks list to the Bookmarks Toolbar.

j. Drag the bookmark **Contractors folder** from the Bookmarks list to the Bookmarks Toolbar.

k. Click **Snipping Tool** in the Accessories folder of the Start menu. You will create a snip of your browser's window.

l. Click the **New snip arrow** and click **Full-screen Snip**.

m. Click File on the menu bar located in the Snipping Tool window and click Save As from the list of File options.

n. Select the drive and folder in which you want to save your image in the Save As dialog box and name the snip **wbr01h3snip1_LastFirst.jpg**.

o. Save and close the JPEG file.

p. Select the Word document *wbr01h3_LastFirst.docx* to make it active.

q. Move the cursor to the end of the Word document and select **Picture** on the Insert tab.

r. Navigate to the *wbr01h3snip1_LastFirst.jpg* file and click **Insert**.

s. Click the **File** and click **Save**. Minimize the window and keep the file open.

STEP 5 ▶▶ DELETE A BOOKMARK

While reviewing Web sites containing statistics for online retail revenue projections, you want to delete a bookmark that is no longer relative to your research. Additionally, you have inquired about funding for a conference and were informed that conferences were not a priority. So you also want to delete the Conferences folder from the Bookmark Toolbar. Refer to Figure 1.33 as you complete Step 5. The folders and bookmarks in your browser's Bookmarks list and the ones in Figure 1.33 will not be identical except for the items created and used in this exercise.

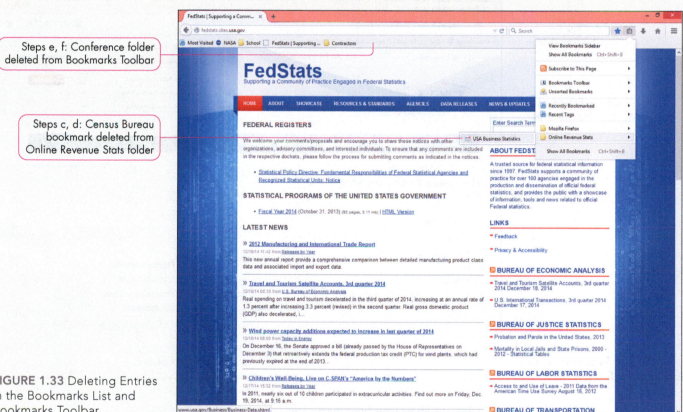

FIGURE 1.33 Deleting Entries in the Bookmarks List and Bookmarks Toolbar

a. Click the **Show your bookmarks icon** to open the Bookmarks list.

b. Display the contents of the Online Revenue Stats folder.

c. Right-click the **Census Bureau bookmark** in the Online Revenue Stats folder.

d. Click **Delete**.

e. Right-click the **Conferences folder** on the Bookmarks Toolbar.

f. Click **Delete**.

g. Click **Snipping Tool** in the Accessories folder of the Start menu. You will create a snip of your browser's window.

h. Click the **New snip arrow** and click **Full-screen Snip**.

i. Click **File** on the menu bar in the Snipping Tool window and click **Save As** from the list of File options.

j. Select the drive and folder in which you want to save your image in the Save As dialog box and name the snip **wbr01h3snip2_LastFirst.jpg**.

k. Save and close the JPEG file.

l. Select the Word document *wbr01h3_LastFirst.docx* to make it active.

m. Move the cursor to the end of the Word document and select **Pictures** on the Insert tab.

n. Navigate to the *wbr01h3snip2_LastFirst.jpg* file and click **Insert**.

o. Click **File** and click **Save**. Minimize the window and keep the file open.

STEP 6 ›› ADD TAGS TO A BOOKMARK

You are getting used to the AutoComplete feature in Firefox's Awesome Bar and want to enhance its accuracy and list of suggestions by adding tags to a bookmark. Refer to Figure 1.34 as you complete Step 6.

FIGURE 1.34 Tags Added to a Bookmark in Firefox

a. Click the **Show your bookmarks icon**.

b. Click the **Online Revenue Stats folder**.

c. Click **USA Business Statistics** within this folder to display the Web page.

d. Click the **Edit this bookmark icon**.

e. Enter the tags *government* and *statistics*, separated by commas, in the **Tags box**.

f. Click **Done**.

You have e-mailed a few members of the project team and asked for input on the social media marketing campaigns that are receiving positive and negative feedback from clients. Additionally, you found that a few competitors have been using Facebook as a marketing tool. You want to create an App tab for your e-mail to keep on top of correspondence and another App tab for Facebook to quickly view notifications. Refer to Figure 1.35 as you complete Step 7.

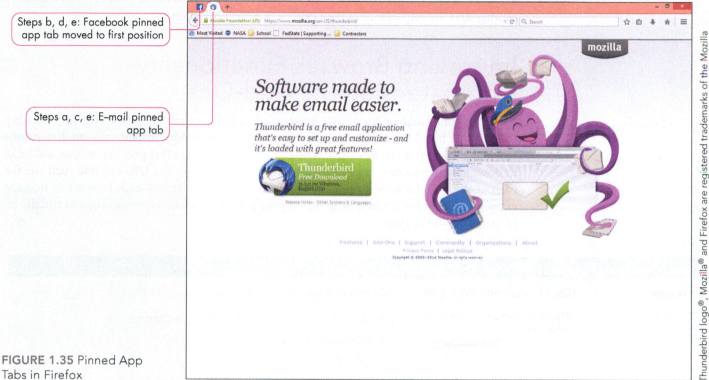

Steps b, d, e: Facebook pinned app tab moved to first position

Steps a, c, e: E–mail pinned app tab

FIGURE 1.35 Pinned App Tabs in Firefox

Thunderbird logo®, Mozilla® and Firefox are registered trademarks of the Mozilla Foundation, Facebook, Inc.

a.   Enter the URL of your e-mail account on the Awesome Bar of a new tab. Press **Enter**.

b.   Press **Ctrl+T** to open a new tab and enter www.facebook.com.

c.   Right-click the tab with your e-mail account and select **Pin Tab**.

d.   Right-click the **Facebook tab**, and then select **Pin Tab**.

   Both tabs are now App tabs located on the left side of the tab row.

e.   Drag the **Facebook App tab** to the left of the App tab with your e-mail so that Facebook becomes the first App tab.

f.   Close any open tabs other than Snapchat and your e-mail. Click **Snipping Tool** in the Accessories folder of the Start menu. You will create a snip of your browser's window.

g.   Click the **New snip arrow** and click **Full-screen Snip**.

h.   Click **File** on the menu bar in the Snipping Tool window and click **Save As** from the list of File options.

i.   Select the drive and folder in which you want to save your image in the Save As dialog box and name the snip **wbr01h3snip3_LastFirst.jpg**.

j.   Save and close the JPEG file.

k.   Select the Word document *wbr01h3_LastFirst.docx* to make it active.

l.   Move the cursor to the end of the Word document and select **Picture** on the Insert tab.

m.   Navigate to the *wbr01h3snip3_LastFirst.jpg* file and click **Insert**.

n.   Click **File** and click **Save**. Submit the file based on your instructor's directions.

o.   Close the browser.

Go Beyond the Basics

After becoming experienced in browsing the Web, there are some browser features that you might want to investigate further. These are the features that go beyond the basics and actually improve the functionality and security provided by the browser, making it more responsive and in tune with your needs.

In this section, you will learn to use extensions or add-ons, identify a secure Web site, and learn about mobile browsers. You also will learn where to locate your browser's security settings and the importance of their review and customization.

Improving Browser Functionality with Extensions or Add-Ons

An *extension* or *add-on* is a simple, browser-specific program that extends the functionality of a browser by adding nonstandard features that enhance your browsing session. Extensions and add-ons are free. There exist several browser-specific sites that provide reviews and links to download extensions and add-ons. Refer to Table 1.15 for the URLs of one such site for each of the popular browsers and the steps to access the menu in each browser to manage extensions or add-ons. Once installed on your system, extensions or add-ons can usually be managed from the menu.

TABLE 1.15   URLs That Provide Browser Extensions

Browser	URL of Extension Web Site	Managing Extensions or Add-Ons	
Chrome	https://chrome.google.com/webstore	<ul><li>Click *Customize and control Google Chrome.*</li><li>Click *More tools.*</li><li>Click *Extensions.*</li><li>Installed extensions will be displayed with options to enable or remove.</li></ul>	Google Inc.
Firefox	https://addons.mozilla.org/en-US/firefox/	<ul><li>Click the *Open menu* button.</li><li>Click *Add-ons.*</li><li>Click *Extensions.*</li><li>The right side of this window will display all installed extensions with options to enable, disable or remove.</li></ul>	Mozilla Firefox
Internet Explorer	http://www.iegallery.com/Add-ons	<ul><li>Click *Tools.*</li><li>Click *Manage add-ons.*</li><li>A Manage Add-ons dialog box opens.</li><li>Right-click an extension, and from the menu that displays, you may choose *Enable* or *Disable.* An extension can also be removed by selecting *More information* from the menu and clicking *Remove.*</li></ul>	
Safari	http://extensions.apple.com/	<ul><li>Click *Safari* on the menu bar.</li><li>Click *Preferences.*</li><li>Click *Extensions.*</li><li>The Extensions window will open with options to enable/disable and remove an extension.</li></ul>	Courtesy of Apple, Inc.

What are some of the capabilities that an extension or add-on can provide? The list is endless; however, a short list of some of the features provided by extensions includes:

- Locating the lowest price for something you want to purchase
- Glancing through Facebook photo albums
- Managing favorites/bookmarks with an extra favorites/bookmarks bar
- Blocking pop-up ads
- Enhancing tab features
- Assisting in speeding up downloads
- Saving form entries into secret memory

STEP 1 ❯ The steps below discuss how to install and remove an extension. The process is very similar in all browsers.

- Type chrome.google.com/webstore in the Address/Location bar and press Enter.
- Click Extensions from the list on the left side of the window.
- Locate and hover over the Google Dictionary extension. (You may need to check *By Google* to further narrow your search.)
- Click + Free (see Figure 1.36).
- Click Add in the Confirm New Extension window.
- The extension displays in the top-right corner of the browser's window to the right of the Omnibox. Right-click the extension's icon to display a shortcut menu. The name of the extension is the first item in this menu (see Figure 1.37).
- To manage extensions in Chrome, refer to the steps in Table 1.15 or right-click the extension and select Manage.

STEP 2 ❯ - The Extensions tab opens in Chrome, and each installed extension is displayed with options to enable and remove (see Figure 1.38).

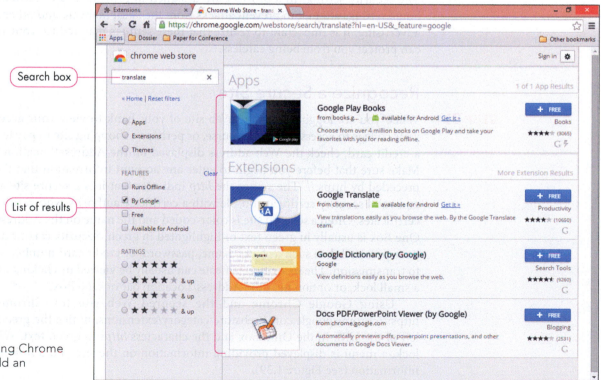

FIGURE 1.36 Using Chrome Web Store to Add an Extension

FIGURE 1.37 Extension in Chrome

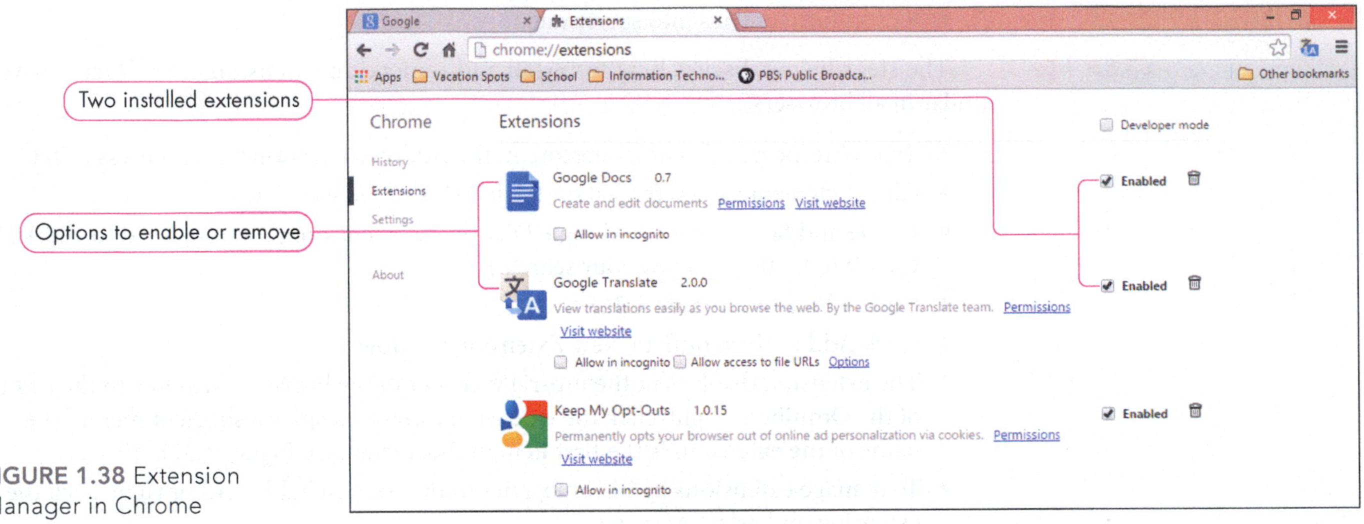

FIGURE 1.38 Extension Manager in Chrome

Reviewing Security Features

The security settings in a browser are designed to provide a safer browsing environment. Some settings attempt to prevent attacks from the latest malware and others try to limit Web advertising. It is important to realize that these settings may reduce your risks, but nothing can protect you from being careless.

Recognize a Secure Site

STEP 3 ▶

When you are logging onto the Web site of your bank to view your account balances, or your college to access an online course, or perhaps a shopping site to pay for a purchase with a credit card, check the Web address displayed on the Address/Location bar or One Box. Make sure that before you begin to enter any account information that the site's address is preceded by https://. The *s* after the *http* indicates that it is a secure site and has a current and valid security certificate on file with a certificate authority who verifies sites and issues certificates. Often a secured site is color-coded and the name on the Address/Location bar or One Box is usually in green text or highlighted in green. Security certificates guarantee that your personal data such as a username, password, or credit card number is encrypted prior to transmission. The security certificate can usually be viewed by clicking on an icon, usually a small lock, or option near the Address/Location bar or One Box.

Using Google Chrome and the secured Web site for Chrome extensions at https://chrome.google.com/webstore/category/extensions, notice the green lock icon to the left of the URL in the Omnibox and the characters *https* in green text. When you click the lock, a menu is displayed providing information on the site and a link to view certificate information (see Figure 1.39).

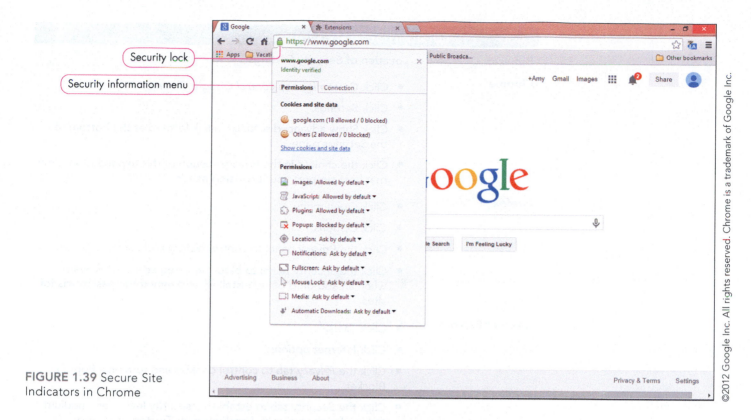

Security lock

Security information menu

FIGURE 1.39 Secure Site Indicators in Chrome

Locate and View Security Settings

Everyone has a different comfort level when browsing the Web. Some security measures such as controlling browser history, setting a notification to warn when multiple tabs are being closed, and restricting third-party cookies have already been covered. Table 1.16 will help you display the security settings in your browser. Review your options and make your choices based on your browsing experience and comfort level.

TABLE 1.16 Locating Security Options

Browser	Location of Security Settings
Chrome	• Click *Customize and control Google Chrome.* • Click *Settings.* • Click Show advanced settings, a link located at the bottom of the Settings page. • Click the choices in the *Privacy* section of this expanded window that best support your browsing needs.
Firefox	• Click *Open menu.* • Click *Options.* • Click the Privacy panel to control history and cookie settings. • Click the Security panel to block reported attack sites, warn when an add-on is being installed, and remember passwords for sites.
Internet Explorer	• Click *Tools.* • Click *Internet options.* • Click the *Privacy tab* to control cookies and turn on a Pop-up Blocker. • Click the *Security tab* to establish a security level from medium to high for the Internet, Local intranet, Trusted sites, and Restricted sites.
Safari	• Click *Safari* on the menu bar. • Click *Preferences.* • Click the Privacy pane to control cookies and other Web site data. • Click the Security pane to activate such options as receiving a warning when visiting a fraudulent Web site, enabling plug-ins, and blocking pop-up windows.

Pop-Up Blockers

Many Web sites use pop-up windows strategically to aid in the functionality of the site, while others use them to bombard the viewer with advertisements. Most browsers have built in pop-up blockers to combat this issue. However, this can have a negative impact if you wanted to view the page being blocked. You can set your pop-up blocker to always allow pop-ups from your favorite sites or to allow them only temporarily. How a browser manages pop-up blocking is different for each browser. In Chrome, for example, the fact that a pop-up was blocked may not be too obvious. A box with a red x will appear in the right side of the Omnibox. See Table 1.17 for managing pop-up blockers. Additionally, it is important to note that any third-party toolbars such as Yahoo Toolbar may also have its own separate pop-up blocker. If you change the settings on the browser and pop-ups are still being blocked for your favorite site, check your toolbar settings as well.

TABLE 1.17	Managing Pop-Up Blocking
Browser	**Location of Pop-Up Blocker Settings**
Chrome	• Click *Customize and control Google Chrome.* • Click *Settings.* • Click Show advanced settings, a link located at the bottom of the Settings page. • Click the *Content settings button* in the *Privacy* section of this expanded window • Scroll to the Pop-ups section and choose the option(s) that best support your needs.
Firefox	• Click *Open menu.* • Click *Options.* • Click the Content panel to control pop-up blocker settings.
Internet Explorer	• Click *Tools.* • Click *Internet options.* • Click the *Pivacy tab* to control pop-up blocker settings.
Safari	• Click *Safari* on the menu bar. • Click *Preferences.* • Click the Security pane to control pop-up blocker settings.

Mobile Browsers

With the number of mobile devices connected to the Internet numbering in the billions, the mobile browser market is an important part of business today. It may also be an important resource in your life as well. A ***mobile browser*** works in much the same way as the browser installed on your computer; however, the Web pages it displays are optimized for reading on a phone, tablet, or other mobile device. The shape and size of the screen as well as the capabilities of the phone or mobile device are a factor. Phones and other mobile devices have smaller memory capacity and lower bandwidth, consequently, the browser software must be optimized to accommodate these characteristics. Moreover, many Web developers design sites specifically for mobile viewing. With these optimized sites, online retailers make it very easy to view and purchase goods. When designing these pages developers need to take into account the most widely used mobile browsers, which differs from those common to computers. Today, the most common mobile browsers are: Safari, Android, and Chrome. With over 50% of the market share, Safari is the most popular browser as it is installed on the most popular mobile phone and tablet, the iPhone and iPad, respectively. Mobile browsers usually come preinstalled with the mobile device. Most people do not choose to install additional browsers on their mobile devices and choose to remain with the default. The third most common browser, Chrome, can be installed on both Android and Apple iOS devices.

Twitter page displayed on iPhone using Safari browser for iPhone

Kennedy/Alamy

Web page displayed on iPad using Safari browser for iPad

IanDagnall/Alamy

FIGURE 1.40 Web pages displayed on phone and tablet

Quick
Concepts

1. What is the purpose of a browser extension or add-on? List a couple of examples. *(p. 48)*

2. How can you recognize whether a site is secure? *(p. 50)*

3. What is the purpose of a pop-up blocker? *(p. 52)*

4. How is a mobile browser different from a computer's browser? *(p. 53)*

Hands-On Exercises

4 Go Beyond the Basics

Google Chrome is the browser that you like to use on your laptop. You have heard that add-ons will make your research more productive. You have decided to download a popular add-on to see if all you have heard about these features is really true. You also want to be able to identify secure Web sites in Google Chrome and check your security settings.

Skills covered: Improving Browser Functionality with Extensions or Add-ons • Removing an Extension or Add-On • Recognize a Secure Site

STEP 1 ▶ **IMPROVING BROWSER FUNCTIONALITY WITH EXTENSIONS OR ADD-ONS**

You recently saw a friend using the Chrome browser and were impressed by a few features that you did not have. When you investigated, you discovered that you both had the same browser version. Your friend informed you that those features were apps, extensions, or add-ons and improved his productivity. You want to give an extension a try to see if it really installs and removes as easily as you've been told and to evaluate its productivity value. Refer to Figure 1.41 as you complete Step 1.

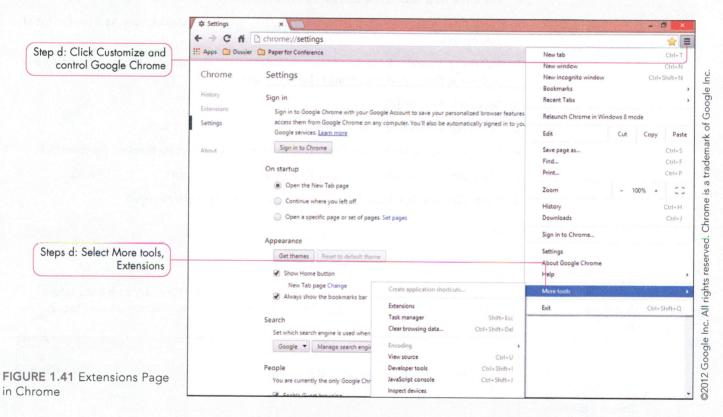

Step d: Click Customize and control Google Chrome

Steps d: Select More tools, Extensions

FIGURE 1.41 Extensions Page in Chrome

a. Start Word. At the top of a blank document, type **Hands-On Exercise 4** and press Enter. On the next line, type *your full name* and the *date*.

b. Save this document as **wbr01h4_LastFirst.docx** and minimize the window.

c. Open **Chrome**.

d. Before installing an extension, it might be helpful to view the Extensions page in Chrome. You might be surprised that several extensions, such as Google Docs, might already be installed without your knowledge. To view the Extensions page, click the **Customize and control Google Chrome icon**, point to **More tools**, and then click **Extensions**.

e. Click **Get more extensions**.

f. Type **Google Dictionary** in the **Search box**. Press **Enter**. This extension, when it is turned on, is designed to allow you to view definitions while you browse the Web.

g. Locate the Google Dictionary (by Google) in the list and click the **+ Free** button. A message will display notifying you what the extension will have access to on your computer and whether to Add or Cancel the extension. Almost anyone can create an extension or add-on for Chrome so it is important to read extension or add-on reviews as well as any information regarding what the extension or add-on will access on your computer.

h. Click **Add**.

i. Locate the dictionary icon indicating that Google Dictionary has been installed successfully. This icon usually appears to the right of the Omnibox. Some extensions or add-ons will want you to restart the browser before the extension or add-on is active.

j. Click to view the Extensions Web page that was already opened previously.

k. Click **Snipping Tool** in the Accessories folder of the Start menu. You will create a snip of your browser's window. You should see the Google Dictionary listed as an extension.

l. Click the **New snip arrow** and click **Full-screen Snip**.

m. Click **File** on the menu bar in the Snipping Tool window and click **Save As** from the list of File options.

n. Select the drive and folder in which you want to save your image in the Save As dialog box and name the snip **wbr01h4snip1_LastFirst.jpg**.

o. Save and close the JPEG file.

p. Select the Word document *wbr01h4_LastFirst.docx* to make it active.

q. Move the cursor to the end of the Word document and select **Pictures** on the Insert tab.

r. Navigate to the *wbr01h4snip1_LastFirst.jpg* file and click **Insert**.

s. Click **File** and click **Save**. Minimize the window and keep the file open.

STEP 2 ›› REMOVE AN EXTENSION OR ADD-ON

After testing the extension that you installed, you want to remove it, and when you have time, try to locate a few extensions that might be more suitable to your browsing behavior. Refer to Figure 1.42 as you complete Step 2.

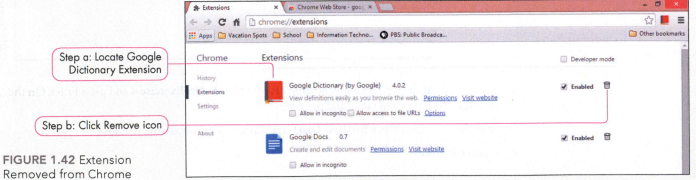

FIGURE 1.42 Extension Removed from Chrome

a. Locate the Google Dictionary add-on in the Extensions Web page. Click the **Remove from Chrome icon** to the right of the Google Dictionary.

b. Use the Snipping Tool to save the JPEG snip of this window as **wbr01h4snip2_LastFirst.jpg**.

c. Make the Word document saved as *wbr01h4_LastFirst.docx* active.

d. Move the cursor to the end of the Word document and select **Pictures** on the Insert tab.

e. Navigate to the *wbr01h4snip2_LastFirst.jpg* file and click **Insert**.

f. Save the *wbr01h4_LastFirst.docx* file. Minimize the window and keep the file open.

g. Close the Extensions tab.

STEP 3 ›› RECOGNIZE A SECURE SITE

You often use your laptop to connect with suppliers and open and review e-mails and online account information from sales representatives. You want to review the security features of Chrome and edit settings that might provide a safer browsing experience. Refer to Figure 1.43 as you complete Step 3.

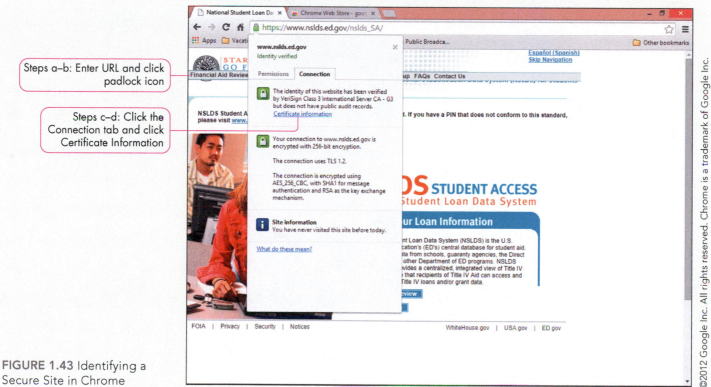

Steps a–b: Enter URL and click padlock icon

Steps c–d: Click the Connection tab and click Certificate Information

FIGURE 1.43 Identifying a Secure Site in Chrome

a. Type **https://www.nslds.ed.gov/nslds_SA/** in the **Omnibox** of the Chrome browser and press **Enter**.

b. Click the **Padlock icon** to the left of the Omnibox.

c. If necessary, Click the **Connection tab** on the window that displays. Notice the displayed message that states *The identity of this website has been verified…*and further states that your connection is encrypted.

d. Click **Certificate information** in the Connection tab to view the issued and expiration dates of the Security Certificate.

e. Display the Word document saved as *wbr01h4_LastFirst.docx*.

f. Move the cursor to the end of the Word document and enter the **issued to** and **valid from** dates of the certificate. Click Ok.

g. Save the *wbr01h4_LastFirst.docx* file, close the document, and submit based on your instructor's directions.

h. Close **Chrome**.

Chapter Objectives Review

After reading this chapter, you have accomplished the following objectives:

1. **Understand how a browser works.**
   - Web pages are developed using established standards, languages, and styles.
   - Web browsers create a seamless connection between the construction and the display of a Web page.

2. **Open and update popular browsers.**
   - The toolkit that Web developers use to create Web pages is constantly being upgraded; browsers that interpret the code created with these tools also need to be upgraded in order to guarantee that the Web page displays true to the developer's intent.
   - Identifying your browser's version and updating it regularly is important for an accurate and error-free browsing experience.

3. **Recognize basic browser features.**
   - Popular browsers have a similar interface and many comparable features such as a Menu button, a Home page button, bookmarks or favorites, an Address/Location bar, a Search bar, Go forward and Go back buttons, a Settings button, a view browser History option, an Open a new tab button, and standards such as scroll bars and the Minimize, Maximize, and Close buttons.
   - Interface features may not be in the same location in each browser, have the same appearance, or become activated in the same way, but they are the features used most often in a browsing session.

4. **Review and change browser settings.**
   - Most browsers have an option or preference setting located off the Menu button, menu bar, or within their tools/customize and control/setting menus to change basic browser settings.
   - The settings most used or edited by users include establishing a home page, activating the option to issue a notification when closing multiple tabs, activating or deactivating browsing history options, restricting third-party cookies, and opening a Private/InPrivate/incognito browsing session.

5. **Become familiar with the favorites or bookmarks feature.**
   - The bookmarks feature enables you to set sites you deem as important in an easy-to-access area that opens the site with just a click of the mouse.
   - To activate, click the site marked as a favorite or bookmark on the favorites/bookmarks bar or in the favorites/bookmarks list and the Web page displays in the browser window without having to remember its URL.

6. **Manage favorites or bookmarks.**
   - The favorites/bookmarks list can get out of control with regard to both length and layout.
   - Related favorites or bookmarks can be grouped and organized into folders for quicker recognition and access.
   - Individual entries in the list as well as folders can be renamed and re-arranged in alphabetical or categorical order.

7. **Explore browser-specific accelerators.**
   - Some browsers have unique features that are usually advertised as being able to accelerate your browsing experience.
   - Tagging is a Firefox feature that helps the AutoComplete feature locate the page and make it display in its suggestion list so you do not have to enter the entire URL.
   - Pinning a tab is a feature of Chrome and Firefox. A pinned tab is anchored to the left side of the tab row and does not have a Close button. It is a feature used most often for sites the update frequently throughout the day.

8. **Improve browser functionality with extensions or add-ons.**
   - Extensions or add-ons are simple, browser-specific programs that extend your browser's functionality and make a browsing session easier.
   - Extensions and add-ons are usually free, are coded for a specific browser, and often install and remove seamlessly.
   - A simple search will provide you with a list and description of extensions or add-ons for a specific browser.

9. **Review security features.**
   - Security settings in a browser are designed to provide a safer browsing environment by preventing attacks from the latest malware and trying to limit Web advertising.

Key Terms Matching

Match the key terms with their definitions. Write the key term letter by the appropriate numbered definition.

a. Add-on
b. Address/Location bar
c. App tab
d. Bookmark/Favorite
e. Browser
f. Browser history
g. Cookie
h. Home page
i. Internet
j. IP address

k. Mobile browser
l. Omnibox
m. Pinned Tab
n. Tab
o. Tag
p. Tear-off tab
q. Uniform Resource Locator (URL)
r. Web server
s. Web site

1. _____ A small text file deposited on your computer by the server on which a Web page you requested is stored or by the server of a Web site that inserts an ad or other element on the Web page you are viewing. **p. 23**

2. _____ A collection of related Web pages. **p. 2**

3. _____ A computer with special software installed that enables it to respond to a browser's request for a Web page. **p. 2**

4. _____ A string of characters that precisely identifies a Web site's type and location; also called a Web address. **p. 8**

5. _____ A Firefox feature that enables you to enter one or more key terms that will then become associated with a bookmark. **p. 37**

6. _____ A browser feature that enables you to drag a tab off of the tab window and release it, making that tab its own browser window. **p. 9**

7. _____ A browser feature that enables you to open multiple Web pages in the same browser window without starting multiple Web sessions. **p. 9**

8. _____ A Web page that is anchored on the left side of the tab row in Firefox and Chrome or on the taskbar in Internet Explorer on a system running Windows 7 or 8. **p. 39**

9. _____ In Chrome, a single text box that performs the actions of the Address/Location bar and Search bar. **p. 8**

10. _____ The box located near the top of the browser's window and the place in which you type a Uniform Resource Locator or Web address. **p. 8**

11. _____ A unique identifying numeric code assigned to your computer by your provider and associated with you for as long as you are logged on to the Internet. **p. 21**

12. _____ A network that consists of thousands of privately and publicly owned computers and networks that grew and interconnected over time. **p. 2**

13. _____ The page automatically displayed when you open your browser; it is set during the installation of the browser and can be changed after installation. **p. 4**

14. _____ A simple, browser-specific program that extends the functionality of a browser by adding nonstandard features that enhance your browsing session. **p. 48**

15. _____ A program stored on your computer that requests a Web page from a Web server, pulls a copy of that Web page over the Internet to your system, and then interprets that page, making it appear in readable form on your screen. **p. 2**

16. _____ The name of a pinned site in Firefox. It has the additional ability to take on a glow effect when the Web site has changed. **p. 39**

17. _____ A file on your hard drive in which every Web page you visit is recorded by your browser. **p. 21**

18. _____ A program stored on a mobile device that requests a Web page from a Web server, pulls a copy of that Web page over the mobile network to your system, and then interprets that page, making it appear in readable form on your device. **p. 31**

19. _____ The use of this browser feature enables you to set sites you visit frequently or deem important in an easy-to-access area that re-opens the site with just a click of the mouse. **p. 31**

Multiple Choice

1. What is the name of the feature located near the top of some browsers' windows that combines the features of the Address/Location bar and the Search bar?

   (a) Title bar

   (b) Omnibox

   (c) Menu bar

   (d) Menu button

2. When a tab is anchored on the left side of the tab row for easy and quick access, it is said to be _____.

   (a) tagged

   (b) a third-party cookie

   (c) a first-party cookie

   (d) pinned

3. Which file on your hard drive contains the record of every Web page you visit?

   (a) Cookie

   (b) Web server

   (c) Browsing history

   (d) Favorites/Bookmarks

4. Which browser feature provides a list of suggestions for phrases or a URL entered in the Address/Location bar?

   (a) AutoComplete

   (b) Favorites/Bookmarks

   (c) Tags

   (d) App tab

5. Which browser is the most common mobile browser?

   (a) Opera

   (b) Firefox

   (c) Internet Explorer

   (d) Safari

6. Which item is a characteristic of a pinned tab?

   (a) The pinned tab is the same size as an unpinned tab.

   (b) Pinned tabs re-display when a new browser session is opened.

   (c) Pinned tabs cannot be repositioned.

   (d) Pinned tabs cannot be closed.

7. Which browser allows tags to be added to a favorite or bookmark?

   (a) Chrome

   (b) Firefox

   (c) Internet Explorer

   (d) Safari

8. All browsers discussed in this text have the following features in common EXCEPT _____. ?

   (a) a box where the Web address can be entered

   (b) the option to pin a tab

   (c) a favorites/bookmark button

   (d) are free to upgrade

9. Which of the following is NOT TRUE about incognito or InPrivate browsing?

   (a) Malicious software may track all of your keystrokes.

   (b) Web sites visited are recorded in your Internet Service Provider's records of your usage.

   (c) Employers are still able to monitor or track your Internet activities.

   (d) Incognito or InPrivate browsing keeps a history of your searches.

10. A small text file deposited on your computer by a Web site other than the one you requested is a _____.

    (a) first-party cookie

    (b) third-party cookie

    (c) bookmark

    (d) tag

Practice Exercises

1 Accessing School-Related Web Sites

You realize that you often visit your college's or university's Web site, your academic e-mail account, the Web page for your major, and your school's academic calendar. You want to make your school's main page your home page, restrict third-party cookies, open separate tabs for the three other school sites that you visit most frequently, create a folder to hold all of your bookmarks related to your academics, and bookmark each site you opened with an identifiable name. Lastly, you would like to pin your academic e-mail tab in order to access it quickly and be well informed of cancellations and notifications issued by the school. This exercise follows the same set of skills as used in Hands-On Exercises 1–3. Refer to Figure 1.44 as you complete this exercise. Your school information will be different than Figure 1.44, but the general browser features such as the number of tabs, bookmarks, and pinned sites will be the same. If a browser other than Chrome is used, your results may look different than those displayed.

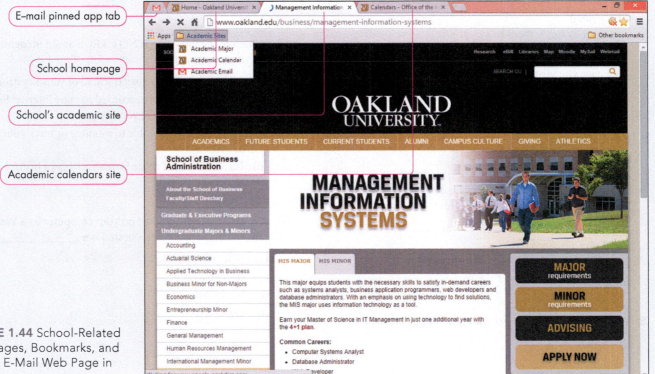

FIGURE 1.44 School-Related Web Pages, Bookmarks, and Pinned E-Mail Web Page in Chrome

a. Start Word. At the top of a blank document, type **Practice Exercise 1**, and then press **Enter**. On the next line, type *your full name* and the *date*. Save this document as **wbr01practice1_LastFirst.docx** and minimize the window.

b. Open the **Chrome** browser. If your browser is already open, close all of the tabs but one.

c. Enter the URL of your school, in the **Omnibox**.

d. Click **Customize and control Google Chrome** and click **Settings**. In the Settings tab, under the On startup section, if necessary, click the button to the left of the Open a specific page or set of pages option. Click the **Set pages** link. The Startup pages dialog box will appear. Click the **Use current pages** button and click **OK**.

e. Use the Snipping Tool to create a JPEG of the Settings tab. Name the snip **wbr01practice1snip1_LastFirst.jpg**.

f. Make the *wbr01practice1_LastFirst.docx* file active.

g. Move the cursor to the end of the Word document and insert the **wbr01practice1snip1_LastFirst. jpg** file.

h. Save the **wbr01practice1_LastFirst.docx** file. Minimize the window and keep the file open.

i. Click **Show advanced settings...** at the bottom of the Settings page. Click **Content settings** in the Privacy section. Click **Block third-party cookies and site data** in the Cookies section.

j. Use the Snipping Tool to create a JPEG of the Privacy section on the Settings page. Name the snip **wbr01practice1snip2_LastFirst.jpg**.

k. Make the *wbr01practice1_LastFirst.docx* file active. Move the cursor to the end of the Word document and insert the **wbr01practice1snip2_LastFirst.jpg** file.

l. Save the **wbr01practice1_LastFirst.docx** file. Minimize the window and keep the file open.

m. You may not wish to block third-party cookies, if not, uncheck the box, and click Done. Close the **Settings tab**.

n. Click **New Tab** or press **Ctrl+T**. In the Omnibox of the new tab, type the URL for your academic e-mail.

o. Open a new tab. In the new tab, enter the URL for the Web page of your major. If you do not know the URL, enter the URL of your school's home page and from the links on that page, locate the Web page of your major or a major that you are interested in pursuing.

p. Open another new tab. In the new tab, enter the URL for the Web page that displays your school's academic calendar. If you do not know the URL, enter the URL of your school's home page and from the links on that page, locate the academic calendar.

q. If *Other bookmarks* is not displayed, click **Customize and control Google Chrome**. Point to **Bookmarks** and click **Show bookmarks bar**.

r. Click **Other bookmarks** on the Bookmarks bar. Right-click in the **Bookmarks list** and click **Add folder** on the shortcut menu. Enter **Academic Sites** in the **Name box**. Click **Save.**

s. Click **Other bookmarks** on the Bookmarks bar. Drag the **Academic Sites folder** so that it is the first item in the Bookmarks list.

t. Click the tab that displays your academic e-mail and click the **Bookmark this page icon**, or if it is already a bookmark, click the **Edit bookmark for this page icon**. Type **Academic Email** in the **Name box** and select the **Academic Sites folder** from the Folder box of the Bookmark added! window. Click **Done**.

u. Repeat the instructions in Step t above and create bookmarks in the Academic Sites folder for both of your other academic pages. Name the site with your major **Academic Major** and the one with the calendar **Academic Calendar**. Then move the Academic Sites bookmark folder to the Bookmarks bar.

v. Re-order the tab row so that your school's home page is first, your academic e-mail is second, the Web page of your major is third, and the academic calendar is fourth. Right-click the e-mail tab and click **Pin tab**. This anchors or pins the e-mail tab to the left of the tab row.

w. Use the Snipping Tool to create a JPEG of the Chrome window with four tabs and the Academic Sites bookmark folder on the Bookmarks bar. Name the snip **wbr01practice1snip3_LastFirst .jpg**.

x. Make the *wbr01practice1_LastFirst.docx* file active. Move the cursor to the end of the Word document and insert the **wbr01practice1snip3_LastFirst.jpg** file.

y. Save and close the file, and submit based on your instructor's directions.

z. Close the Chrome browser.

2 Planning a Vacation

You and your family are planning a vacation to Paris, France, and you want to start researching airfares, hotels, and tours there. You want to create a bookmark folder for your trip and tag and place relevant bookmarks into this folder. You also want to verify that the airlines you are considering have a secured Web site, and you want to make your e-mail site a Pin tab. Some of the Web sites you find are in French so you add a Google Translate extension to help translate the pages. This exercise will follow the same set of skills as used in Hands-On Exercises 1–4. Refer to Figure 1.45 as you complete this exercise. Your travel sites will be different than Figure 1.45 but the general browser features such as the number of tabs, bookmarks, extensions, and pinned sites will be the same. If a browser other than Chrome is used, your results may not display identical to those displayed.

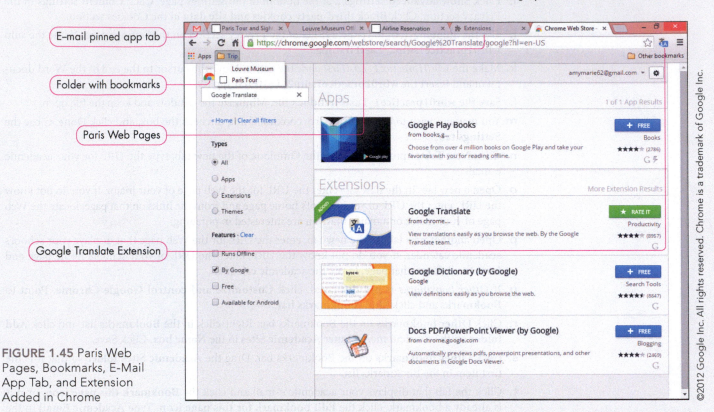

E-mail pinned app tab

Folder with bookmarks

Paris Web Pages

Google Translate Extension

FIGURE 1.45 Paris Web Pages, Bookmarks, E-Mail App Tab, and Extension Added in Chrome

a. Start Word. At the top of a blank document, type **Practice Exercise 2** and press **Enter**. On the next line, type *your full name* and the *date and press* **Enter**. Save this document as **wbr01practice2_LastFirst.docx** and minimize the window.

b. Open **Chrome**. Click the **Customize and control Google Chrome icon**, click **About Google Chrome**. In the *wbr01practice2_LastFirst.docx* file, type **Google Browser Version:**, and then type the browser's version. Save and minimize the **wbr01practice2_LastFirst.docx** file.

c. Close the **About** tab. If Other bookmarks is not displayed, click **Customize and control Google Chrome**. Point to **Bookmarks** and click **Show bookmarks bar.**

d. Type **Paris tours** in the **Omnibox**. Locate a Web site that contains information on Paris tours. When you locate a link, right-click the link and from the shortcut menu, select **Open link in new tab.** Your first result will open in a new tab, while still keeping your search results.

e. Click the tab with the original Paris tours search results. Type **Louvre Museum** in the **Omnibox**. Open the link that appears to be most relevant to the search.

f. Click **Other bookmarks** on the Bookmarks bar. Right-click in the **Bookmarks list** and click **Add folder** on the shortcut menu. Enter **Trip** in the **Name box**. Click **Save.**

g. Click the **Paris tours tab** and click the **Bookmark this page icon**. Click the **Edit this bookmark icon.** Change the name in the Name box to *Paris Tours*. Select the **Trip folder** from the drop-down menu, and then click **Done.**

h. Click the **Louvre tab** and click the **Bookmark this page icon**. Click the **Edit this bookmark icon.** Change the name in the Name box to *Louvre Museum*. Select the **Trip folder** (if necessary) from the drop-down menu, and then click **Done.**

i. Open a **new tab**. Open the Web site of an airline that flies to Paris (such as American Airlines). Select your departure and return dates. Continue to book your flight all the way to the Web page of the airline in which your name and credit card is to be entered. Confirm that this is a secure site by locating the https:// in front of the URL on the Address/Location bar. Keep this third tab open.

j. In a new tab, open the e-mail account that you are going to use to receive information about your trip, such as flight confirmations. Right-click your e-mail tab and select **Pin tab**.

k. Use the Snipping Tool to create a JPEG of the Chrome window with four tabs. Name the snip **wbr01practice2snip1_LastFirst.jpg**.

l. Make the *wbr01practice2_LastFirst.docx* file active. Move the cursor to the end of the Word document and insert the **wbr01practice2snip1_LastFirst.jpg** file.

m. Save the **wbr01practice2_LastFirst.docx** file. Minimize the window and keep the file open.

n. Click the **Customize and control Google Chrome icon**, click **Settings**. A new tab will open. Click **Extensions**. Click **Get more extensions** (located at the bottom of the extensions list).

o. Type **Google Translate** in the Search box. Select **By Google** in the Features list.

p. Locate the Google Translate and click the **+ Free button** to add the extension. Click **Add**. Click the **Extensions** tab to view the newly added Extension.

q. Use the Snipping Tool to create a JPEG of the Extensions tab with Google Translate visible. Name the snip **wbr01practice2snip2_LastFirst.jpg**.

r. Make the *wbr01practice2_LastFirst.docx* active. Move the cursor to the end of the Word document and insert the **wbr01practice2snip2_LastFirst.jpg** file.

s. Save the **wbr01practice2_LastFirst.docx** file, close the file, and submit as directed by your instructor.

t. Close the Chrome browser.

Mid-Level Exercises

1 Locating Restaurants

FROM SCRATCH

You have recently moved and want to locate, bookmark, and add tags to three restaurants that serve and deliver pizza in your new neighborhood. Using the Firefox browser, enable the saving of browsing history and notification when closing multiple tabs. Open and use Google Maps to locate directions to the restaurant you seem to favor.

a. Start Word and type **Mid-Level Exercise 1**. On the next line, type *your full name* and the *date*. Save as **wbr01midex1_LastFirst.docx**.

b. Open the Firefox browser.

c. Enable the saving of browsing history.

d. Use the Snipping Tool to create a JPEG of the screen displaying the settings for browsing history and another JPEG of the options showing that the warning for closing multiple tabs has been activated. Name the JPEG files **wbr01midex1snip1_LastFirst.jpg** and **wbr01midex1snip2_LastFirst.jpg**.

e. Insert both JPEG files into the *wbr01midex1_LastFirst.docx* file after your name and date.

f. Create a favorites/bookmarks folder labeled **Eating Out**.

g. Locate the Web sites of three restaurants in your neighborhood that provide the food and services that you like. Bookmark each site, assigning an appropriate name to each, saving each in the Eating Out folder.

h. Display the favorites/bookmarks bar.

i. Drag the **Eating Out folder** from the favorites/bookmarks list to the favorites/bookmarks bar.

j. Type **http://maps.google.com** in a new tab on the Address/Location bar.

k. Pin the Google Maps tab.

l. Use the Snipping Tool to create a JPEG of the screen displaying the favorites/bookmarks bar and the Pinned Google Maps tab (if your browser has this feature). Name the JPEG file **wbr01midex1snip3_LastFirst.jpg**.

m. Insert the JPEG file into the *wbr01midex1_LastFirst.docx* file after snip 2.

n. Save, close, and submit the file based on your instructor's directions.

2 Keeping Track of Sports Teams

FROM SCRATCH

You have just joined a fantasy football league with some of the students in your class and want to research a few teams and some players before your league's draft. First, you want enable the option to receive a warning when closing multiple tabs and reject third-party cookies. Then, you want to set the NFL's main page as your home page and bookmark a few Web sites that will provide you with current information on team and individual athlete's statistics. All related fantasy league bookmarks will be in a Football folder that displays on your favorites/bookmarks bar. Use the Firefox browser to add a few appropriate tags to each bookmarked site. Locate a sports site and add bookmarks on the bookmarks toolbar.

a. Start Word and type **Mid-Level Exercise 2**. On the next line, type *your full name* and the *date*. Save as **wbr01midex2_LastFirst.docx**.

b. Open the Firefox browser.

c. Enable the option to receive a warning when closing multiple tabs and reject third-party cookies.

d. Use the Snipping Tool to create a JPEG of the screen displaying the enabling of a warning when closing multiple tabs and another JPEG of the screen setting that shows the setting not to accept third-party cookies. Name these JPEG files **wbr01midex2snip1_LastFirst.jpg** and **wbr01midex2snip2_LastFirst.jpg**.

e. Insert both JPEG files into the *wbr01midex2_LastFirst.docx* file after your name and date. Save and minimize this file.

f. Type **http://www.nfl.com** and make this page your home page.

g. Use the Snipping Tool to create a JPEG of the Options/Settings screen, displaying the nfl.com page as the home page. Name this JPEG file **wbr01midex2snip3_LastFirst.jpg**.

h. Insert this JPEG file into the *wbr01midex2_LastFirst.docx* after snip 2.

i. Create a Bookmarks folder labeled **Fantasy Football**.

j. Locate two additional Web sites containing information on NFL football teams or statistics. Bookmark each site with an appropriate name and tag (if using Firefox). Save each bookmark in the Fantasy Football folder created in step i.

k. Display the Favorites/Bookmarks bar.

l. Move the Fantasy Football folder from the Bookmarks list to the **Bookmarks toolbar**.

m. Type **http://espn.go.com/nfl/** in a new tab on the Address/Location bar.

n. Pin the tab for the ESPN NFL Web page.

o. Create a JPEG of the browser window displaying the ESPN NFL tab pinned (if your browser has this feature) and the favorites/bookmarks bar displayed containing a Fantasy Football folder. Name this JPEG file **wbr01midex2snip4_LastFirst.jpg**.

p. Insert this JPEG file into the *wbr01midex2_LastFirst.docx* file after snip 3. Save, close, and submit based on your instructor's directions.

Beyond the Classroom

The Movies

GENERAL CASE ✓

You are a movie buff and enjoy reading reviews of movies both before and after you view them. Open your favorite browser and search for a Web site of a movie critic such as Roger Ebert. Make the Web site of your chosen movie critic your home page. Create a bookmark folder labeled **Movie Reviews** and place in this folder two bookmarked sites that you appropriately named and tagged (if your browser has this feature). Display the favorites/bookmarks bar and move the Movie Review folder to that toolbar. Since all your friends know how much you enjoy keeping up with current movie releases, you are always getting Facebook notices and e-mails with movies they have viewed. Open your e-mail and Facebook pages and pin both sites, if this feature is available in your browser. If not, rearrange the tabs so that your e-mail tab is first and Facebook is second.

Open a Word document and on the first line, type the title **Beyond the Classroom—The Movies**. On the second line, type *your full name* and the *date*. Save the Word document as **wbr01beyondmovies_LastFirst.docx**. Use the Snipping Tool to create the snips below and insert them into the Word document in the order listed. Save the Word document, close, and submit as indicated by your instructor.

- **wbr01beyondmoviessnip1_LastFirst.jpg**: A snip displaying the Options dialog box of your browser with the home page set to that of a movie review site.
- **wbr01beyondmoviessnip2_LastFirst.jpg**: A snip displaying the Movie Reviews folder on the favorites/bookmarks bar.
- **wbr01beyondmoviessnip3_LastFirst.jpg**: A snip displaying pinned e-mail and Facebook tabs or the tabs in the order specified in the instructions.

The Cost of Higher Education

RESEARCH CASE

Attending college has become quite an expensive endeavor. Although financial aid is available, college can be an expense that seems overwhelming. Open your favorite browser and make your current school your home page. Make sure third-party cookies are disabled. Create a favorites/bookmarks folder labeled **College Information**. Locate, bookmark, and tag one Web site with information on the cost of higher education. Save this bookmark in the College Information folder. Locate one government-sponsored secure Web site for student loans and bookmark it in the College Information bookmark folder. Move the College Information bookmark folder to the favorites/bookmarks bar. Locate a Web site related to the cost of higher education. Save this site as a bookmark on the favorites/bookmarks bar. Lastly, locate an add-on compatible with your browser that enables additional features for either tabs or your search bar. Install and enable this add-on.

Open a Word document and on the first line, type the title **Beyond the Classroom—Higher Education**. On the second line, type *your full name* and the *date*. Save the Word document as **wbr01beyondeducation_LastFirst.docx**. Use the Snipping Tool to create the snips below and insert them into the Word document in the order listed. Save the Word document, close, and submit as indicated by your instructor.

- **wbr01beyondclasssnip1_LastFirst.jpg**: A snip displaying the Options dialog box of your browser with the home page set to the home page of your school.
- **wbr01beyondclasssnip2_LastFirst.jpg**: A snip displaying the Options dialog box of your browser with the option to not accept third-party cookies displayed.
- **wbr01beyondclasssnip3_LastFirst.jpg**: A snip displaying the College Information favorites/bookmarks folder and the bookmark for the site on the favorites/bookmarks bar.
- **wbr01beyondclasssnip4_LastFirst.jpg**: A snip displaying the Add-ons Manager with a tab or search add-on displayed.

Job Search

SOFT SKILLS CASE S

FROM SCRATCH

Graduation is fast approaching and you have begun your job search. You begin researching potential companies and organizations in your field. In your search you will locate at least three companies as well as two job board Web sites. Using your browser, add a favorites folder titled *Job Search* and place bookmarks to those companies inside the folder. Using the Snipping Tool take a snip of the folder with the three companies inside. (To take a Windows snip using the Snipping Tool of a menu, open the

Snipping Tool, then open the menu to display the folder and sites, finally press CTRL+PrntScr to take the snip.) Add your snip to a new blank Word document. Add the job board sites to the bookmarks bar and then take a Windows snip showing the job board sites. Save the document as **wbr01beyondjobs_ LastFirst** and submit as directed by your instructor.

- **wbr01beyondjobssnip1_LastFirst.jpg**: A snip displaying the Job Search folder with the three companies inside.
- **wbr01beyondjobssnip2_LastFirst.jpg**: A snip displaying the two job board sites on the book-marks bar.

Capstone Exercise

You are the new assistant to the director of Human Resources for a legal firm and have been given the responsibility to locate flights for employees who need to travel. Because some travel is last minute, you want to improve your efficiency by making your home page the page of the airline you use most frequently. Your e-mail should be a pinned tab so that it is easy to access. Additionally, you want to bookmark a few hotel Web sites and place those bookmarks in a folder labeled Hotels. If your browser permit tagging, insert appropriate tags for your hotel bookmarks. Lastly, you want to locate and install an add-on for coloring your tabs in the browser that you are using. Once your browser is set up, locating and booking airline and hotel reservations will be effortless.

Open a Browser and Change Settings

a. Start Word. At the top of a blank document, type **Capstone Exercise**. On the next line, type *your full name* and the *date*. Save this document as **wbr01cap_LastFirst. docx** and minimize the window.

b. Open your browser.

c. Make the home page a local airline.

d. Use the Snipping Tool to create a JPEG of the screen displaying the home page URL. Name the JPEG file **wbr01capsnip1_LastFirst.jpg**.

e. Insert this JPEG file into the *wbr01cap_LastFirst.docx file* after your name and date. Save and minimize the file.

Create, Manage, and Tag Favorites/ Bookmarks

a. Create a Bookmarks folder labeled **Hotels** in the favorites/bookmarks list.

b. Locate two hotel Web sites. Bookmark each site using an identifiable name, save the bookmarks in the Hotels folder in the favorites/bookmarks list, and if your browser has the option to tag a bookmark, insert at least one tag for each bookmark.

c. Display the favorites/bookmarks bar and move the Hotel folder to the favorites/bookmarks bar.

d. Use the Snipping Tool to create a JPEG of the browser screen with the favorites/bookmarks bar displayed. Name this JPEG file **wbr01capsnip2_LastFirst.jpg**.

e. Insert the JPEG file into the *wbr01cap_LastFirst.docx file* after snip 1. Save and minimize the file.

Pin Tabs to Accelerate Browsing

a. Open your e-mail account. Pin the e-mail tab to the left of the row of tabs.

b. Use the Snipping Tool to create a JPEG of the browser screen with the Favorites/Bookmarks bar displayed. Name this JPEG file **wbr01capsnip3_LastFirst.jpg**.

c. Insert the JPEG file into the *wbr01cap_LastFirst.docx file* after snip 2. Save and minimize this file.

Install an Add-On

a. Open a new tab and use your favorite search engine to locate a browser compatible add-on of your choice.

b. Install the add-on.

c. View the window that manages the add-ons in your browser to confirm the add-on is installed and enabled.

d. Use the Snipping Tool to create a JPEG of the browser screen with the Add-on Manager window open and the favorites/bookmarks bar displayed. Name this JPEG file **wbr01capsnip4_LastFirst.jpg**.

e. Insert the JPEG file into the *wbr01cap_LastFirst.docx file* after snip 3. Save, close, and submit the file as indicated by your instructor.

Glossary

Add-on A simple, browser-specific program that extends the functionality of a browser by adding nonstandard features that enhance your browsing session.

Address/Location bar The box located near the top of the browser's window and the place in which you type a Uniform Resource Locator or Web address.

App tab The name of a pinned site in Firefox. It has the additional ability to take on a glow effect when the Web site has changed.

Awesome Bar A more current name for the Address/Location bar in Firefox due to its ability to remember Web sites you have gone to and make suggestions as to where you want to go.

Bookmark The use of this browser feature enables you to set sites you visit frequently or deem important in an easy-to-access area that re-opens the site with just a click of the mouse.

Browser A program stored on your computer that requests a Web page from a Web server, pulls a copy of that Web page over the Internet to your system, and then interprets that page, making it appear in readable form on your screen.

Browser history A file on your hard drive in which every Web page you visit is recorded by your browser.

Cookie A small text file deposited on your computer by the server on which a Web page you requested is stored or by the server of a Web site that inserts an ad or other element on the Web page you are viewing.

Extension A simple, browser-specific program that extends the functionality of a browser by adding nonstandard features that enhance your browsing session.

Favorite The use of this browser feature enables you to set sites you visit frequently or deem important in an easy-to-access area that re-opens the site with just a click of the mouse.

Favorites/bookmarks bar A bar that can be displayed near the top of a browser's window and contains individual Web pages you have marked as favorites or bookmarks, icons for folders that represent categories into which you have organized some of your favorite/bookmarked Web pages, and browser-specific options.

First-party cookie A cookie generated by a Web site you requested to view.

Home page The page automatically displayed when you open your browser; it is set during the installation of the browser and can be changed after installation.

Internet A network that consists of thousands of privately and publicly owned computers and networks that grew and interconnected over time.

Internet Service Provider (ISP) A company that provides access to the Internet.

IP address A unique identifying numeric code assigned to you by your provider and associated with you for as long as you are logged on to the Internet.

Menu bar A horizontal bar positioned across the top of the browser window that contains commands such as File, Edit, View, History, Bookmarks, Tools, and Help.

Menu button An orange button, unique to Firefox, that replaces the menu bar and is located in the top-left corner of the browser's window. When the Menu button is clicked, a menu displaying additional options appears.

Omnibox In Chrome, a single text box that performs the actions of the Address/Location bar and Search bar.

One Box In Internet Explorer, a single text box that performs the actions of the Address/Location bar and Search bar.

Pinned A Web site is pinned when it is anchored on the left side of the tab row in Firefox and Chrome or on the taskbar in Internet Explorer on a system running Windows 7.

Search bar A text box located near the top of a browser's window, usually to the right of the Address/Location bar, in which you enter words or strings of words related to the Web search you are performing.

Tab A browser feature that enables you to open multiple Web pages in the same browser window without starting multiple Web sessions. A tab identifies each opened Web page, and all tabs are aligned in one row near the top of the browser window.

Tag A Firefox feature that enables you to enter one or more key terms that will then become associated with a bookmark.

Tear-off tabs A browser feature that enables you to drag a tab off of the tab window and release it, making that tab its own browser window.

Third-party cookie A cookie generated by a Web site other than the one you requested.

Title bar The top thick border of the browser's window.

Uniform Resource Locator (URL) A string of characters that precisely identifies a Web site's type and location; also called a Web address.

Web The general term for the content available over the Internet.

Web page An individual document or resource, created using established standards, which is transported over the Internet.

Web server A computer with special software installed that enables it to respond to a browser's request for a Web page.

Web site A collection of related Web pages.

Index

A

accelerate browsing, 31–40. *See also* browsing
  bookmarks feature, 31–35
  exploring browser-specific accelerators, 37–40
  managing favorites or bookmarks, 35–37
add-ons, 48
  defined, 48
  improving browser functionality with, 48–50
Address/Location bar, 8
AJAX (Asynchronous JavaScript and XML), 2
Amazon, 23
Android, 53
App tab, 39
Asynchronous JavaScript and XML (AJAX), 2
Awesome Bar, 8

B

bookmarked Web pages, 33–34
browser extensions. *See* extensions
browsers
  activating privacy (incognito or InPrivate) browsing, 21–23
  basic features, 7–10
  defined, 2
  downloading, 4
  history, 21
  icons associated with popular, 4
  identifying version of, 4–6
  improving functionality with extensions or add-ons, 48–50
  introduction to, 2–10
  locating and viewing security settings, 51–52
  managing history of, 21
  mobile, 53
  opening, 3–4
  personalizing, 15–24
  popular, 4
  pop-up blockers, 52–53
  restrict cookies, 23–24
  reviewing and changing settings of, 15–24
  reviewing security features, 50–54
  updating an existing, 4
  working of, 2
browser screen elements
  Address/Location bar, 8
  Awesome Bar, 8
  menu bar, 7

  Omnibox, 8
  One Box, 8
  Search bar, 8
  title bar, 7
  Uniform Resource Locator (URL), 8
browser-specific accelerators, 37–40
  pinning a Web page, 39–40
  tagging a Web page in Firefox, 37–39
browsing
  accelerate, 31–40
  history, 21
  incognito, 21–23
  InPrivate, 21–22
  private, 21–22

C

Cascading Style Sheets (CSS), 2
cookies, 15
  defined, 23
  first-party, 23
  restricting, 23
  settings, 24
  third-party, 23
  usual concerns about, 23
CSS (Cascading Style Sheets), 2
Customize and control Google Chrome button, 5

E

extensions, 48
  Chrome Web Store, using to add an, 49
  defined, 48
  improving browser functionality with, 48–50
  URLs, providing, 48

F

Facebook, 39, 49
FactorX, 1
favorites/bookmarks
  becoming familiar with, 31–35
  deleting, 37
  icon, 31
  making, 31
  making folders, 36
  managing, 35–37
  organizing, 35–36
  renaming pages or folders, 36–37
favorites/bookmarks bar, 31
  customizing, 34–35
  viewing, 31–33
Firefox, 39
  adding tags to bookmarks in, 37

  Awesome Bar in, 8
  creating tags in, 38
  options window, 17
  tagging a Web pages, 37–39
first-party cookies, 23

G

Gmail, 39
Google Account, 15
Google Chrome
  bookmarks list, 34
  changing home pages in, 18
  extension in, 50
  extension manager, 50
  pinned sites in, 40
  screen elements in, 8
  secure site indicators, 51
  settings Web page, 16
  window close protector extension, 20

H

home pages
  defined, 4
  setting, 17–19
HTML, 2

I

incognito browsing, 21–23. *See also* browsing
InPrivate browsing, 21–22. *See also* browsing
Internet, 2
Internet Explorer, 4, 8–9, 39
Internet service provider, 4
IP address, 21

J

JavaScript, 2

L

languages
  scripting, 2
  Web programming, 2

M

menu bar, 5, 7
Menu button, 21
Menu button commands, 21
mobile browsers, 53–54. *See also* browsers
Mozilla Firefox. *See* Firefox

O

Omnibar, 8
Omnibox, 8
One Box, 8

P

pinned Web sites, 39. *See also* Web sites
pop-up blockers, 52–53
private browsing, 21–22. *See also*
    browsing

S

Safari, 4, 6, 8–9, 15, 19, 31–32
scripting languages, 2
Search bar, 8

T

tabs, 9
    making use of, 9–10

multiple, 19–21
    opening additional, 9
    tear-off, 9
tags, 37
    creating, in Firefox, 38
    purpose of, 37
tear-off tabs, 9. *See also* tabs
third-party cookies, 23
title bar, 7, 10
Twitter, 39

U

Uniform Resource Locator (URL), *See*
    Web addresses
providing browser extensions, 48

W

Web, defined, 2
Web addresses, 8
Web pages
    defined, 2

locating and opening favorites or
    bookmarks, 33–34
    pinning, 39–40
    settings in Chrome, 16
    tagging in Firefox, 37–39
Web programming
    languages, 2
Web server, 2
Web sites
    defined, 2
    pinned, 39
    pinning, 40
    recognizing secure sites, 50–51

X

XHR (XMLHttpRequest), 2
XML, 2
XMLHttpRequest (XHR), 2